NOMADIC?

rover by days singing these
gang plank songs of the ambler

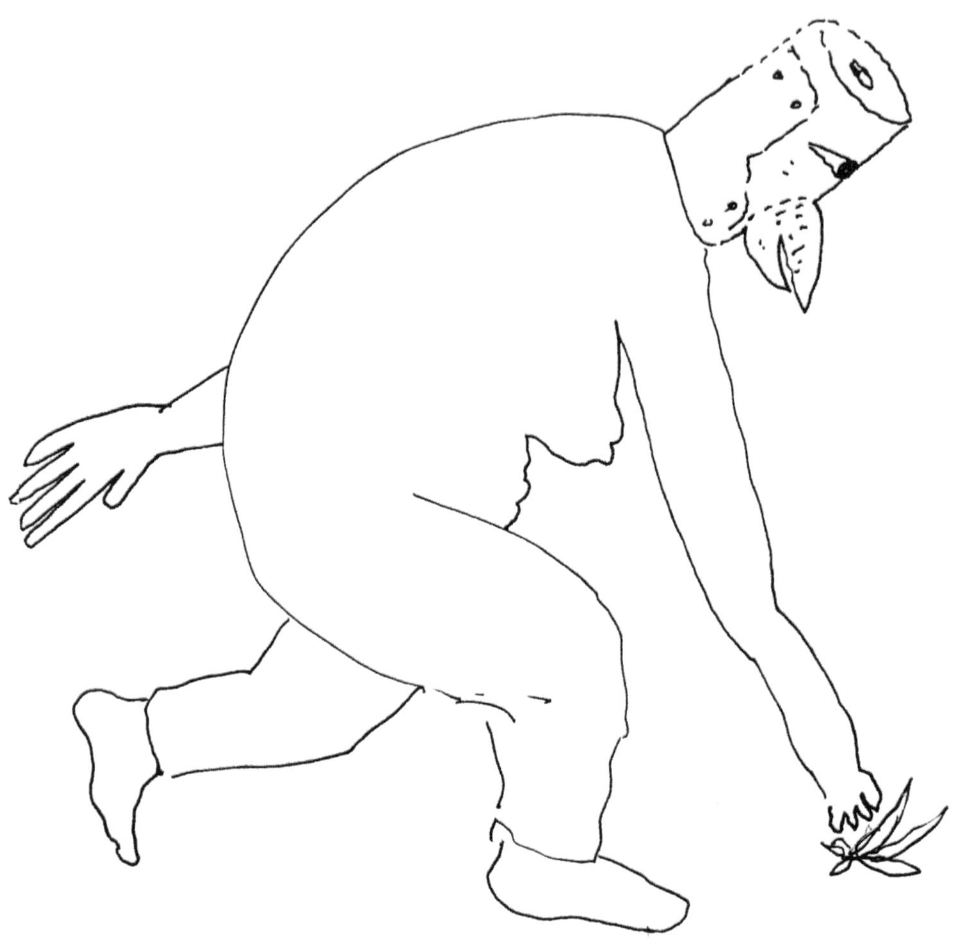

also by Hugh Merrill

the birth of christ

the victory at bullrun

the kennedy assassination

the loss of virginity of rosie

Preaching to the Choir

NOMADIC?

rover by days singing these
gang plank songs of the ambler

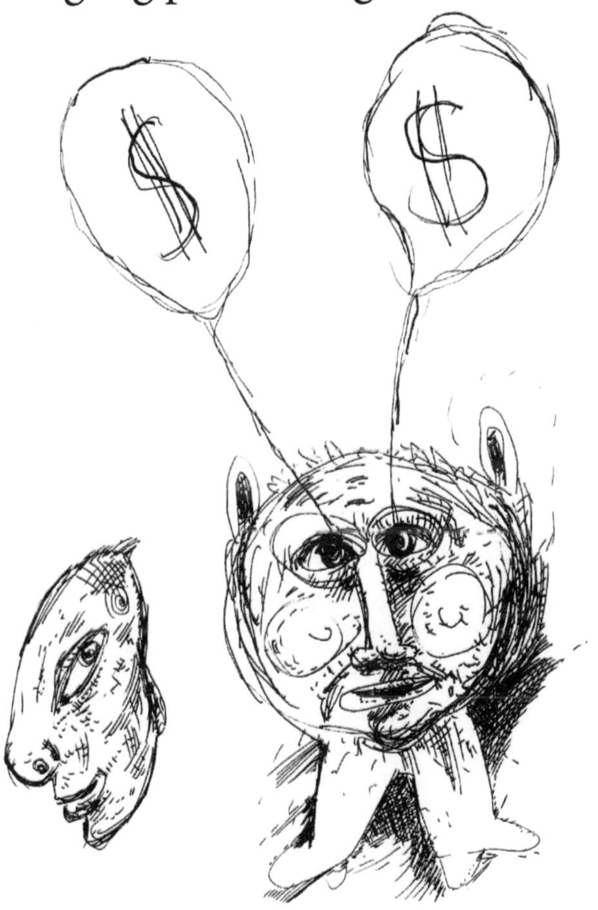

poems by

Hugh Merrill

39 WEST
PRESS

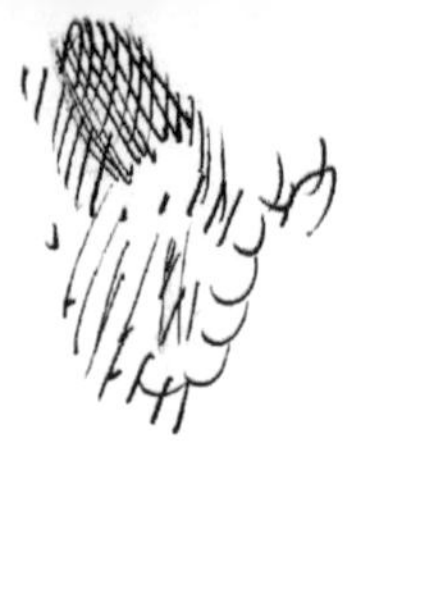

39 WEST PRESS
Kansas City, MO
www.39WestPress.com

39 WEST
PRESS

First Edition: August 2016

ISBN: 978-0-9908649-5-0

Library of Congress Control Number: 2016947066

10 9 8 7 6 5 4 3 2

Design & Layout: Jeanette Powers
Edits: Jeanette Powers & j.d.tulloch
Cover & Interior Art: Hugh Merrill

39WP-12

CONTENTS

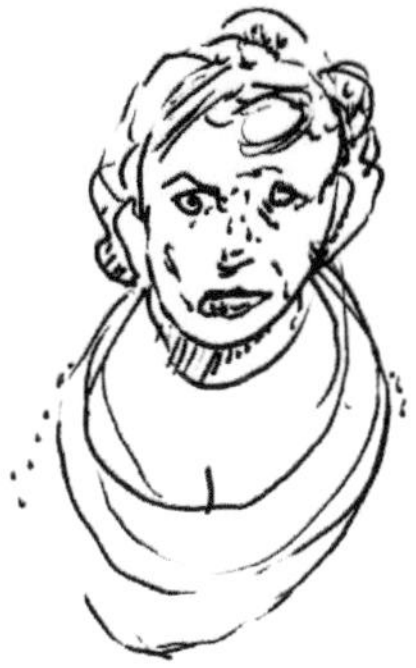

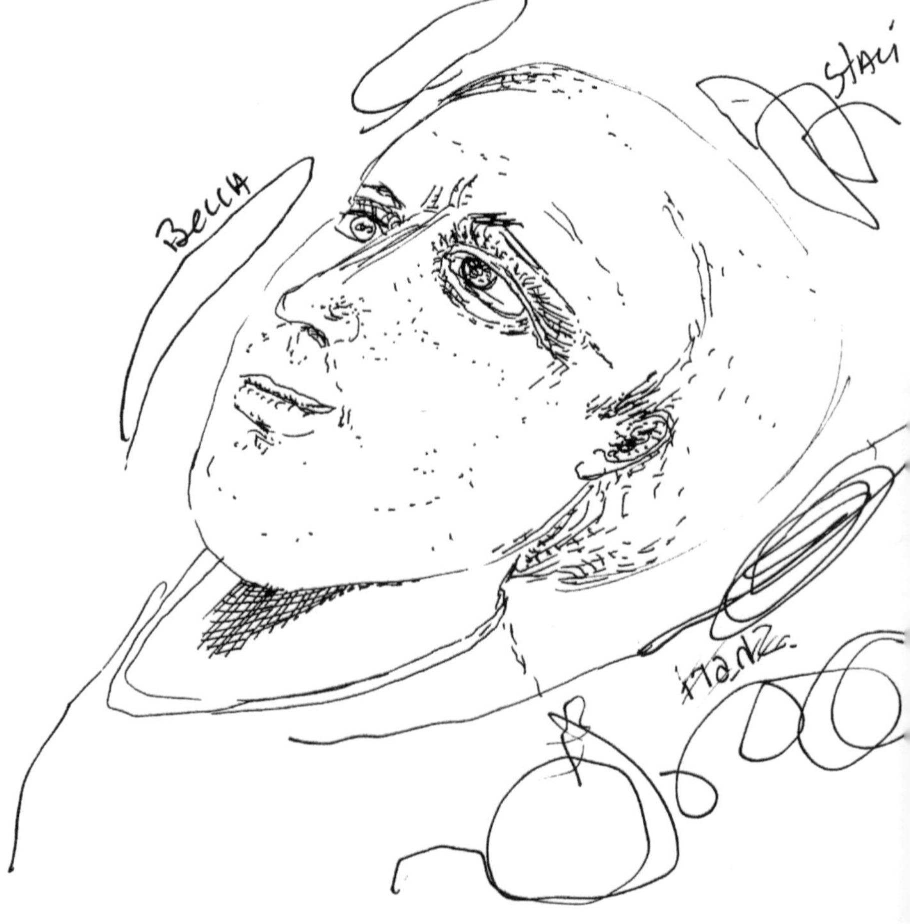
Becca
Staci

For my friend and mentor, Jeanette, and the amazing poetry folks at the ARTS BAR and Prospero's Books, Kansas City.

ACKNOWLEDGMENTS

In 1968, I hung out with Allen Ginsberg and his friends, Manny Navarrete and John Cage, in the studio where I lived, drew, and painted. They seemed to like my paintings. So, as a 20-year-old feeling very bold, I handed Ginsberg my sketchbook containing a new poem I had written. He took it, adjusted his glasses, and read the poem to himself, twice. I waited expectantly. Finally, he handed me the notebook and said only one word: *PAINT.* Manny and Cage broke into laughter, as did I. Ginsberg was kindly telling me to focus, and I did. But quietly, I kept writing, and at the age of 67, I am pleased to work with the amazing, Jeanette Powers and 39 West Press to publish my first book of poetry.

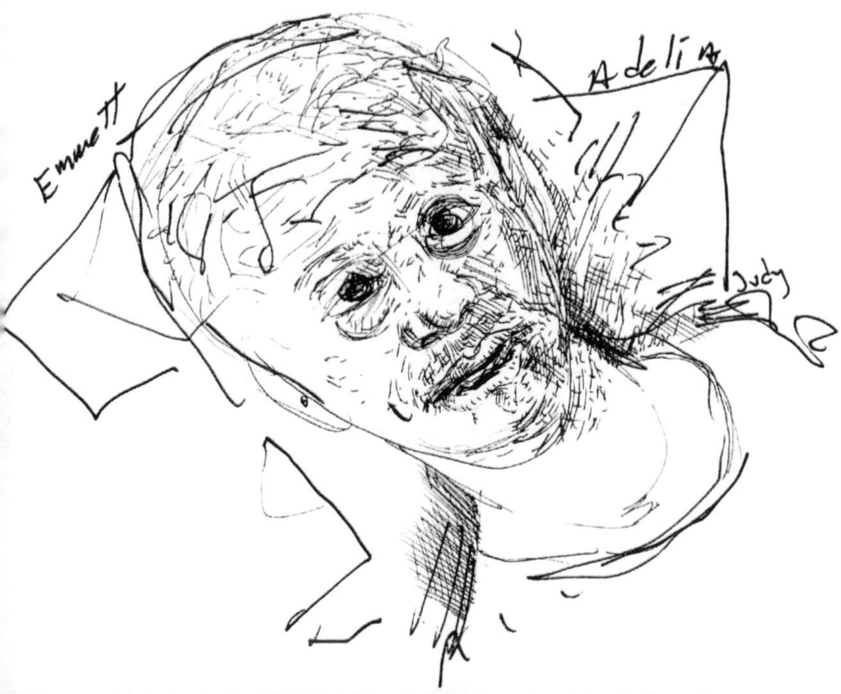

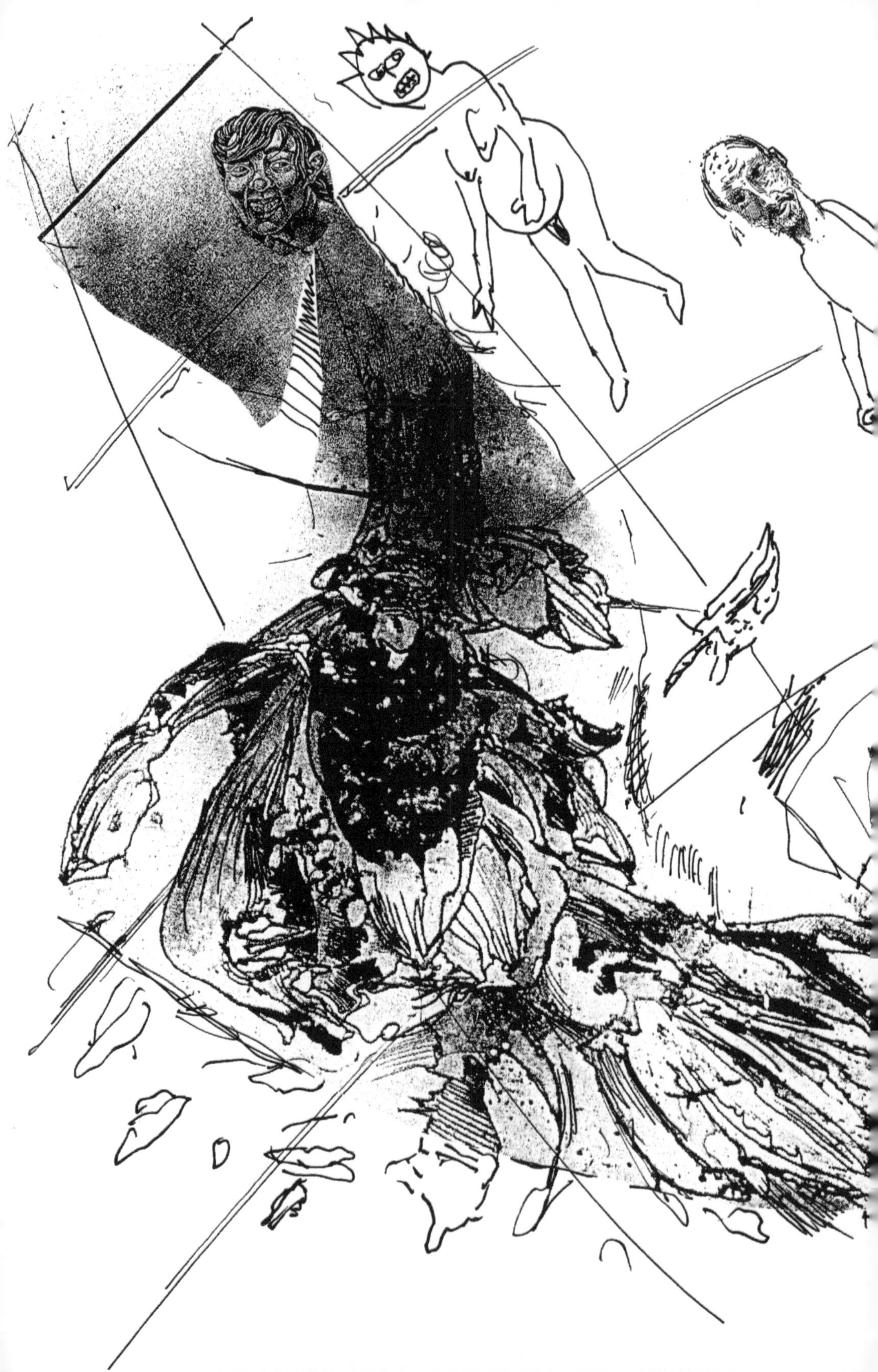

BIRTH STORY

Jordan was dead when he finally squirted free from Evelyn's birth canal. Her thoughts were wild with fear but not for the loss of the child she had hated for the past eight months. It had been six years since the birth of her last child, a morose little boy whose eyes haunted her and whose hypersensitivity kept her on constant edge.

The silence of the rural clinic was wonderful and appropriate for the birthing of a silent infant. The newborn lay small, blue, wet and bloody on the sheets between his mother's legs.

There were two beds in the clinic, and if the scene were viewed from the location of the ceiling light bulb at the instance of Jordan's birth, you would have seen a sweaty and exhausted beauty. A woman of 32, propped up by several pillows, lay spread-eagle on the clinic bed. Her hospital gown had fallen open, exposing her firm breasts and white skin. She had a look of pain, yet relief, on her refined face, which was framed by wet and matted reddish-brown hair. Her covers had fallen to the floor between the bed and the window that looked out on the cow pasture surrounding the clinic on three sides.

Her husband, Jim, and the doctor sat on the second bed, drunk on Old Crow. Smoke hung in the seemingly thick air. At the very instant the blue baby finally emerged and fell onto the bed, they leaned forward, spilling the full ashtray perched between them. The oversized, glass receptacle smashed onto the floor of the infirmary, breaking the silence for an instant, but no one seemed shocked by the sound.

Velma, the nurse, stood at the foot of the bed holding a dry towel. Her right foot bounced, waiting for the doctor to finally hand her the newborn baby. The room was still, except for the smoke rising from the stub of a cigarette in Doctor Asher's mouth and the one between the fingers of the father. As they leaned forward to look at the baby, their glasses of Old Crow tilted to the spilling point.

Doctor Asher's brain suddenly engaged, and he rushed forward with knowledge and proficiency. He grabbed the dead baby by the feet and yanked up Jordan with such force that his placenta was suddenly pulled down the birth canal, following the same path as the child. He held the baby upside down by the feet with his left hand and reached back with his right hand to grab the half-full bottle of Old Crow. He poured the bourbon over the child, and with several strong whacks to the back and rump, the child came alive, coughing up yellowish phlegm that splattered over his mother's belly and crotch.

She looked at the small boy in astonished wonder. The anguish of perpetual guilt that would undermine the child for decades to come could be seen in her eyes.

BARROOM MIRROR

Why sing without talent, without a voice?
why speak without knowledge, without cause?
Why go on without hope
with the taste of soles on the tongue?

I sing for money, the pretty boy cried.
I sing for fame, the cat chimed.
All is ego, over and over again, croaked the moaning frog.
The invisible author of my sulfur scented songs
left scratching secret verses in an unknown alphabet
ends shouting out a cruel bird's mating call.

Why sing without talent, without a voice
spending nights drinking down illusions
glimpsing in the mirror, mumbling
please go, please just sleep?

BUY BUY

Not interrupted by the whistle of immeasurable time
never worn down, or blown to the sea
the drone of hungry voices, the TV does not stop

nor the baying mules, selling useless life styles
flower mouths selling toilet paper
philosopher puppets being authentic and truthful.

The mysterious is motionless
submissive souls, extinguished reality
a crop of humans to buy and buy.

The *I* you call me is created by them
never the *I made myself I*
the silent one

told again and again
(not to speak)
shut up

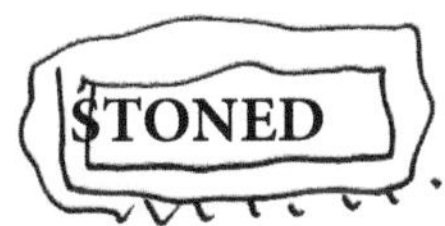

STONED

I rode away from their churches
past their garrisons of empty enchantments
not glimpsing myself in their dark waters of belief
they are distrustful of me
from their devil's words
to their stones hitting my face
devoured by religion
sitting in a circle facing east
creating forms of oblivion I do not prefer
soaked with sweat, blood and fatigue
impoverished under their unforgiving clamor
I died in darkness
only a stoned illusion

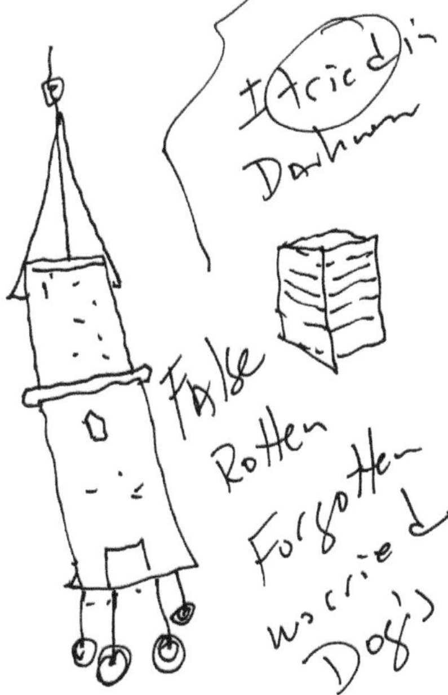

a lie eth Devil's
words

SEEDS AND THORNS

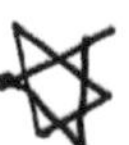

A thousand mornings wasted in another man's fields
bustling booms between legs scratched raw
the erotic violet light of dawn consuming night's flames.
The sun lights the sleeping bundle pleasantly
a uniform of naked disgust, worn heavy by this child
forward, a day filled with seeds and thorns.
The Negro wakes to catch the bus across town
an ancient being, a slave
once sleeping free under the stars
a statue with a thousand bodies and one mind.

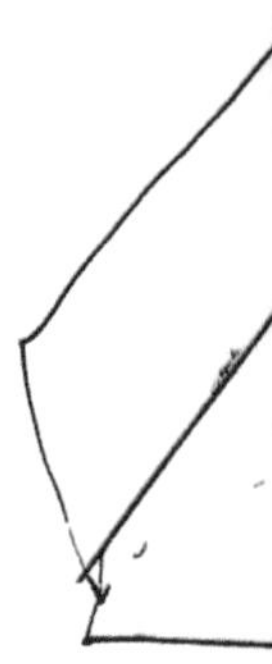

Oh great statue, shivering in mad solitude
swimming in oceans of strong tides, misdirected.
This hemisphere's shores are close and freedom lies.

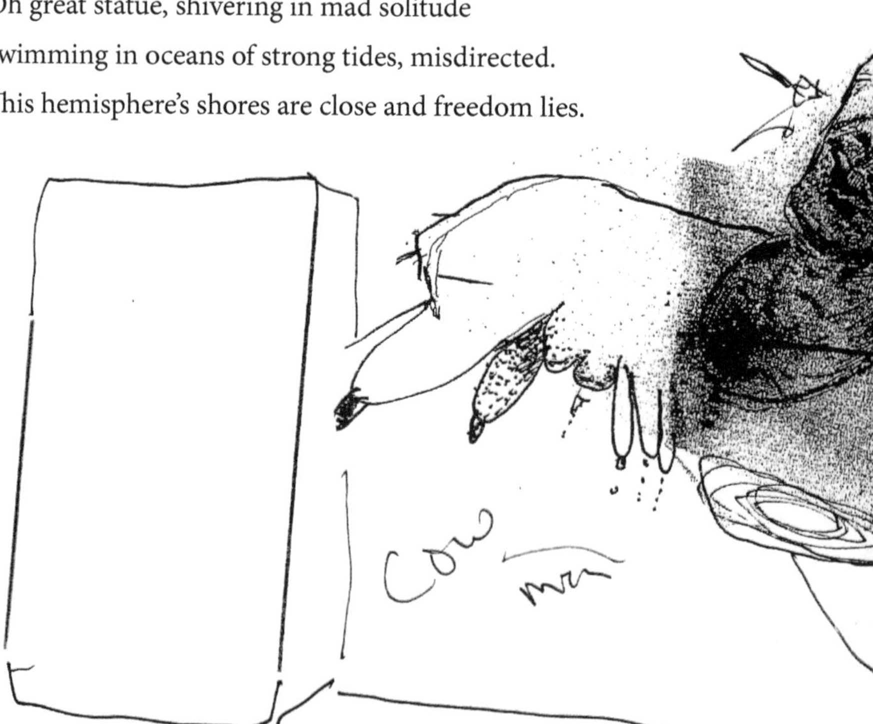

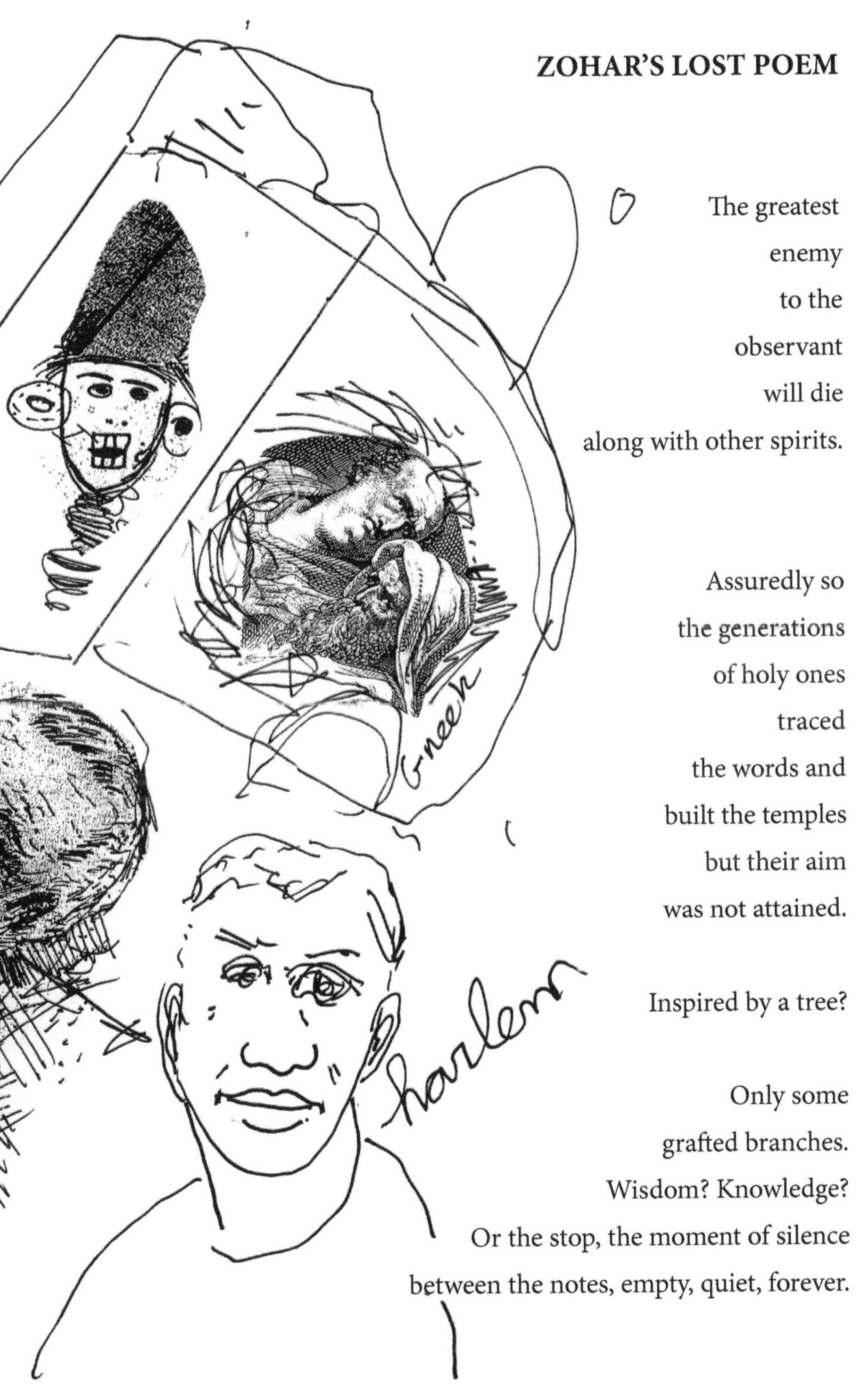

ZOHAR'S LOST POEM

O The greatest
enemy
to the
observant
will die
along with other spirits.

Assuredly so
the generations
of holy ones
traced
the words and
built the temples
but their aim
was not attained.

Inspired by a tree?

Only some
grafted branches.
Wisdom? Knowledge?
Or the stop, the moment of silence
between the notes, empty, quiet, forever.

THE PARTY

Let's eat properly now, the party is over!

Instantly her eyes are heavenly
not sleeping, not dreaming.
Lips are soundless, our body hums distantly.
We cannot be, we have no past and we have no future:.
We part, still entangled, into the scent
of the palpitating mist.

The rain cycle?

Time to disappear, only to fall again.
Our buckets filled to the brim by quick encounters
with the serpent's invisible hand the pails are tipped.
We return to our burrows, satiated yet unfulfilled
wet and shivering this treasure
is lost in the wave of a hand.

From the old mother's black tit, nothing drops but time.

Leaving only a vacant lot without nests,
where are we overcome by silence?

THE PARTY (answer song by JP)

eat properly now
your party is over

instantly her eyes are heavenly not sleeping not dreaming
lips are soundless body hums distantly
we cannot be: we have no past
and we have no future

we part entangled
mist palpitates
rain disappears
sweat returns

these body casks fill so quickly
serpent's invisible mouth tipping our pail
we burrow alone: satiated and unfulfilled

from the old mother's black tit
nothing drops but time
leaving only a vacant lot
where we
are overcome
by silence

THE SECOND COMING?

In the madness of swimming up stream
we smash our bodies on mountains of igneous rock.
Detached and left dead, picked over, rotting flesh
having fallen to pieces, our impurity consumed
like a candle lighting; a candle, lighting a candle
until not a soul remains.

Only in this vibrating emptiness, primordial fates rest
watch by day and by night for the energy of harmony.
The solitude of potential, sleeping
in waters of foam and pop bottles.

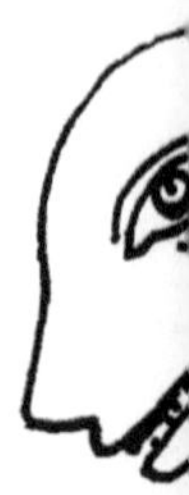

The power hovering in the mist, just out of sight.

The frustration of waiting internally, gliding
a coin unspent
ready to be used again, a lie of resurrections.

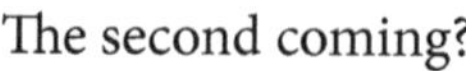

The second coming?

No! Only all consuming oneness.

ON DOING THE WASH

she worked full time as a secretary

the trembling of the river
musically lifting a branch from the shoreline
my lover came in to hover over me

drifting rain, losing the light of day, howling
and there goes the cell phone
buzzing like the vibrator's joy
small birds scream confused, *the cat?*
or just the smell of burning rubbish

Richard enters the office, looking
like a sailor proud of his ship
the earth stretches like a black sea
hiding stories a century old

I am middle class
went to a suburban high school
colors were blue and gold

the sea birds, grey
dancing at the edge of foam and sand

God I went through
thick and thin to get this audition

the ocean's roaring call
the gentle lion and the dark faltering pines

I lift my dirty panties
and drop them into the washing machine

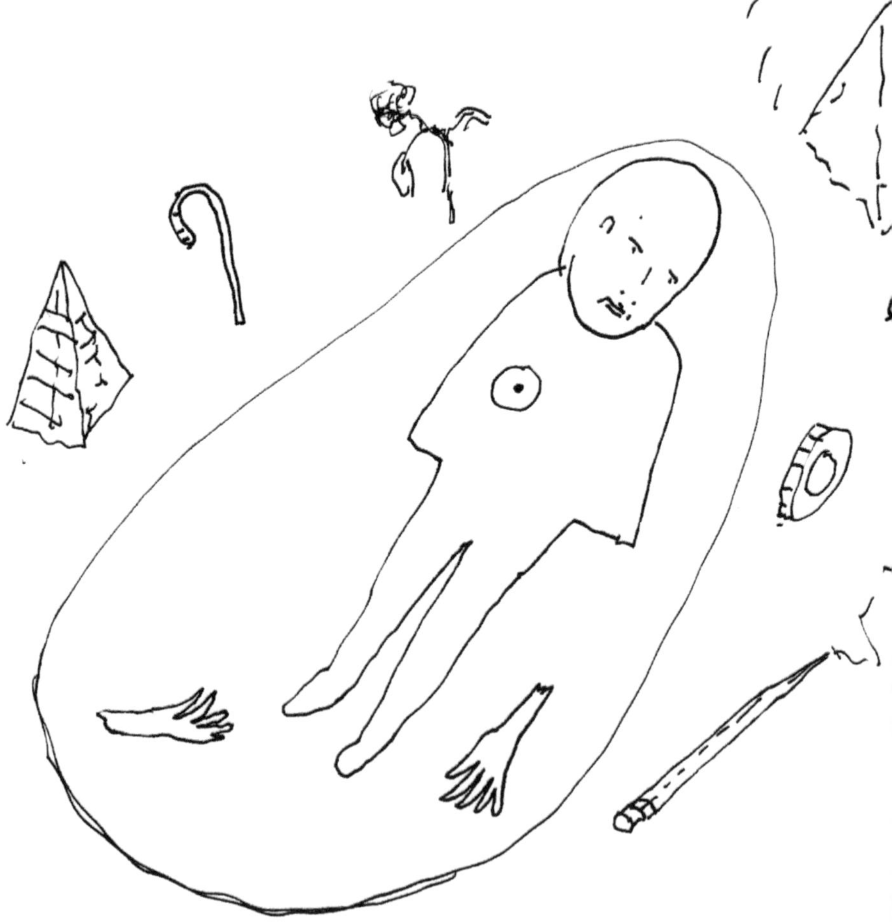

KICKING THE CAN

making important decisions
to buy razors online or at the pharmacy
carefully she wipes the mirror
but it simply fogs again
trust the mind
the clear intellect
or follow the fog of the heart?

these twins were never identical
marked by degrees of differentiation
without love or hate her legs opened
receiving nothing but a hard on
gears shift to neutral
seeking emptiness
mmmmmmmmmm she moans

she dreams of winning a game of kick the can
of not being skipped over but picked
the fathers tell lies of a life embracing all
but some are always left behind
dreaming of a space
of no phenomena
and no names or titles

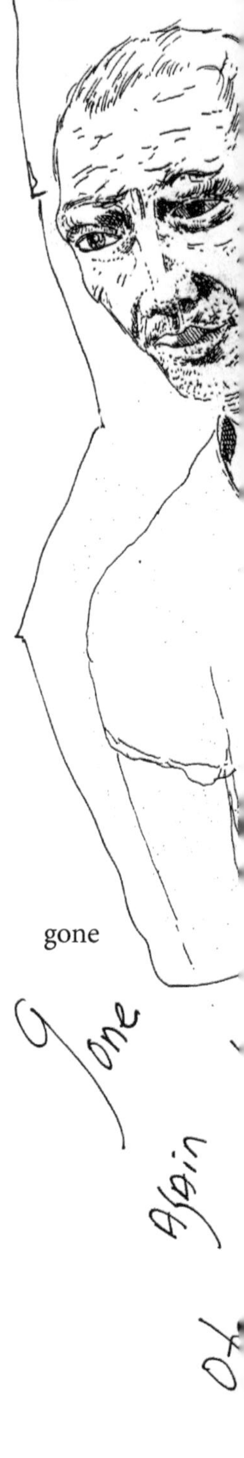

AN ONLY UNQUENCHABLE THIRST

it was you that gave birth to me and I gave birth to you
a night of glistening breasts
tits if you wish
wild penetrations into nature and our nothingness

it was you that gave birth to me and I gave birth to you
a red stain, resembling celestial meat
now gapes and displays the gory crown
blood turns to whine (whining)

it was you that gave birth to me and I gave birth to you
white hills eroded, empty goblets and absence
sleeping fitfully, breathing a sigh (of relief?)
she has run dry, drained into an only empty ocean gone

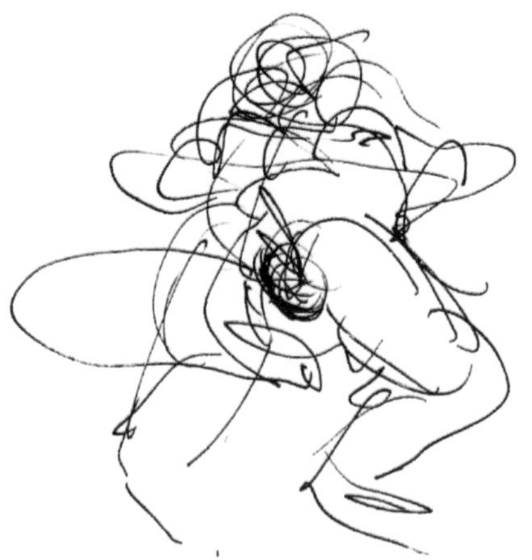

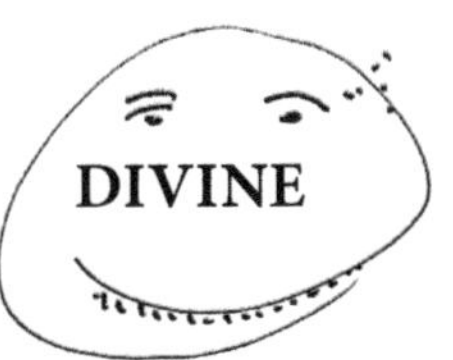

DIVINE

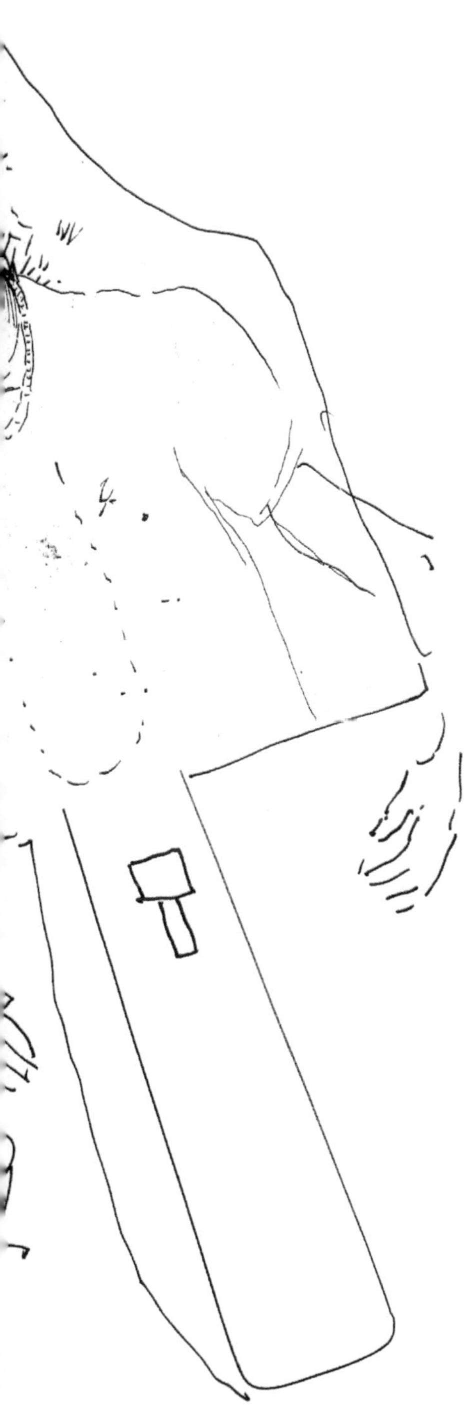

they all had been drinking
obscenities. they spat at her.
she was their river, their lives.
she now ran dry, draining
into the empty ocean
dead fish eyes, is this seeing?
first the birds left, followed
by herds, ghosts that could not
get out. lead poisoned children
laughing without memory.
distorted heads feeding in
the womb of infected mothers.
now, children and criminals
take refuge here on this day.
the beast swoops down,
destroyer of worlds, never killing
the bad bums first.
tender was the cry
of the lion leaving
the carcass behind:
so fat, so very fat with the meat
of the green earth. bones, left for
dead like white coral, the *madre*
des les madres will return unseen.

THE DRUNK PSALMIST

I transgressed once, twice; again and again
but was punished for other sins
I rejoiced over cedar arrows that cut their skin
I cried and begged for our feet to stand at the gates
Let us go
we wandered, rejoicing and bringing them all down
the sweet sojourn
I cried, *draw swords*
but in the midst of violence
the baths of horror overwhelmed me

I have long considered how all wounds healed not
the small river of life, only a wash of words
binding mine eyes; word is pure, word is deep
word is truth   word   word
word is all

they kept not thy word to be merciful
hath never suffered so, and shall reward evil
not far from me the king of joy
sets down a crown of pure wickedness

give ear not to thyself
and cut off the truth

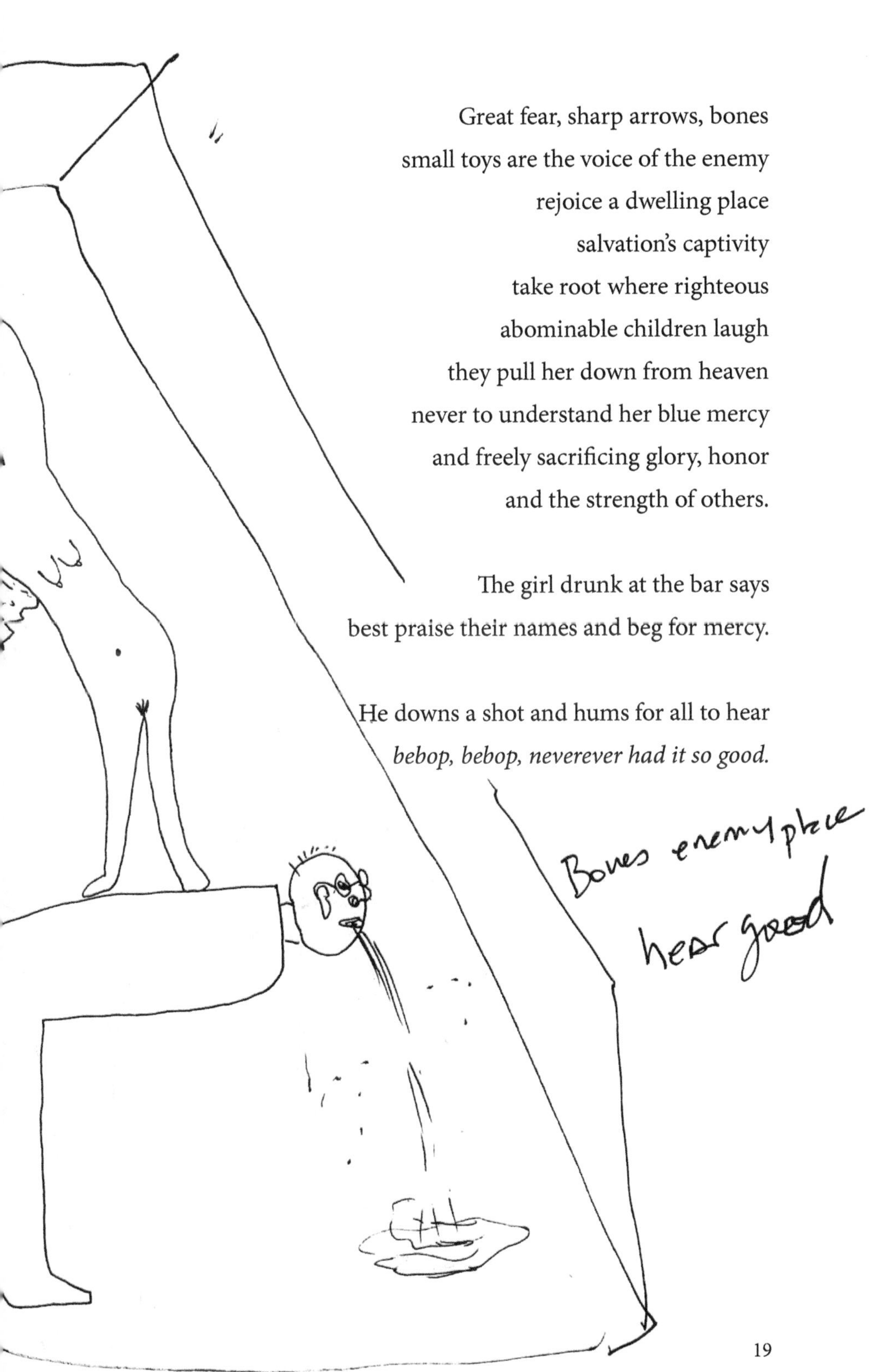

Great fear, sharp arrows, bones
small toys are the voice of the enemy
rejoice a dwelling place
salvation's captivity
take root where righteous
abominable children laugh
they pull her down from heaven
never to understand her blue mercy
and freely sacrificing glory, honor
and the strength of others.

The girl drunk at the bar says
best praise their names and beg for mercy.

He downs a shot and hums for all to hear
bebop, bebop, neverever had it so good.

MAKE STORY

Notes to J.P.

When I make my visual art works, there is no narrative, no center, no expression of an idea. There is only reaction to the surface of the paper and the marks and colors, the space created by me and the drawing materials. Yet there are personal stories, historical, political, scientific and faith based resources that determine the making of the work. But because I know so little, I cannot make a pronouncement and say this is what I am saying. I live the works more than make them. From this mess of thought that makes up my life, the poetry is written, as are the stories.

I flunked most of my classes in elementary and high school, also college and so on. I did get degrees, but it was the 1960s, so ...

When I write, I am outside myself, and images and words come in sequences and have little to do with each other from one line to the next. I form them so that they make sense to me like my abstract paintings do. There is a little bit of a story, but no conclusion, or the real conclusion is a false understanding by me and the audience. I have no deep meaning to tell the audience, yet the poems have depth: like diving deeper, the pressure grows. No matter what the diver sees or thinks, the pressure grows. I do not want to say the "something." There are no grand conclusions, but my poems are interesting and have a heart. They may be best performed, so that the audience can hear the words but cannot slowly think about them, as when they are read. And like all writers, I would like to publish them. It is my life and work; it is what I do.

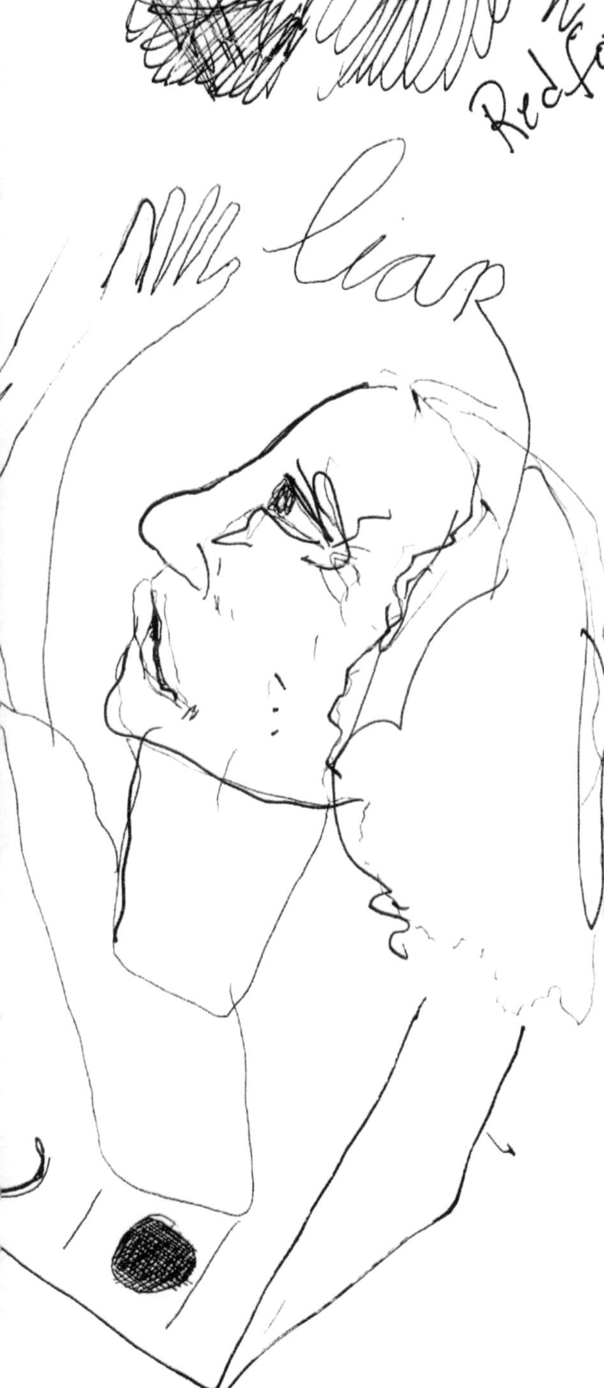

FUNNY

A voice in the night
yo Lenny Bruce
gone dead funny
a little traveling music
cell phone playing
around midnight
a jazz joke
on the Metro cruse-ing
a white collar warrior
in a rocker bar
waiting for an offer
spatter and splatter
sex and a fight
as always no winners
flashing blue
and red lights
cops and bull shit
the bar closes
the nasty leave last.

Life is a
steady gig
of sorrow
and relief.

GOLD OF CENTRAL AMERICA IN THE HEAD OF YOUR NEIGHBOR

Hypocrisy is a question of degree chimed Ron Reagan
our president
our killer.
Let the dust fly
the mountain people of Central America
in newly named countries
they died
not Reagan's problem
not a tear shed but commies held at bay.
I guess
anyway
I am bored and into my own head
I like to walk bare foot and look at necklaces
dress like a weird Guatemalan, play the man of the native people
no blood, no relation but it is hip and cool I did a sweat lodge
in my back yard once
I know
I read Don Juan.
Your culture is owned, me and mine
change is coming, but not for you
your cool the way I want you to be
stay cool brother, stay cool
it is not up to you
a bought and sold life style is gold

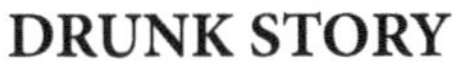

DRUNK STORY

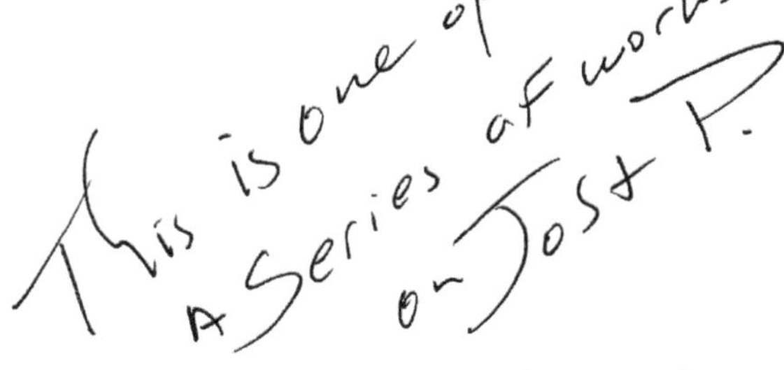

Job had been down on his luck when he meant Pandora. Pandora, a new mother at 38, was the enthusiastic director of a do-gooders agency. She had been out fighting social injustice till she was sick of everyone and everything.

The bar was empty, dark and cool. The outside deck still had several office workers lingering over a late lunch and early cocktails. Job swiveled on his barstool to get a better look at the middle-aged woman standing in the door. Pandora paused in the entrance of the bar to let her eyes adjust to the darkness. Through the dim light, she saw a man sitting by himself at the bar. She pulled at the hem of her skirt and walked directly to him, taking the seat next to his.

With the curtains drawn, Job's hotel room was as dark as a tomb. Even after several hours, their eyes were seeing only their inner thoughts. Pandora rolled over, cupped her left breast with one hand and guided it to Job's sleeping mouth. She heard him softly moan and felt his tears roll down her breast, mixing with her sweet milk. *The food of the Gods,* she mused.

He stayed in bed while she fumbled with her bra and got dressed. The baby was at her sister's; she had planned to work late. Now, she had that feeling of guilt and success: the duality of kicking ass and being dragged down into the judgmental abyss. Perhaps when she opened the door to the room, this time, only hope would enter her world.

SPOON

I am a junkie
each morning I sit
with last night's streams
coming through my ears and eyes
all I can think about is the next stuff.

David held the spoon
my hand shook
as I cooked my way out
sunrise, a new day
but not for me.

Noon and scuffling
on the street
he pulled up my skirt
as I sat on the vinyl seats
of his Ford Galaxy.

I spit never swallow
only swallow for those I love
small measures make
a big difference
between being
and not to be.

Shaked like
Shit—
I remembered this
well—walking uptown
Baltimore
at Sunrise Acid &
Downers—good music
And a past out friend

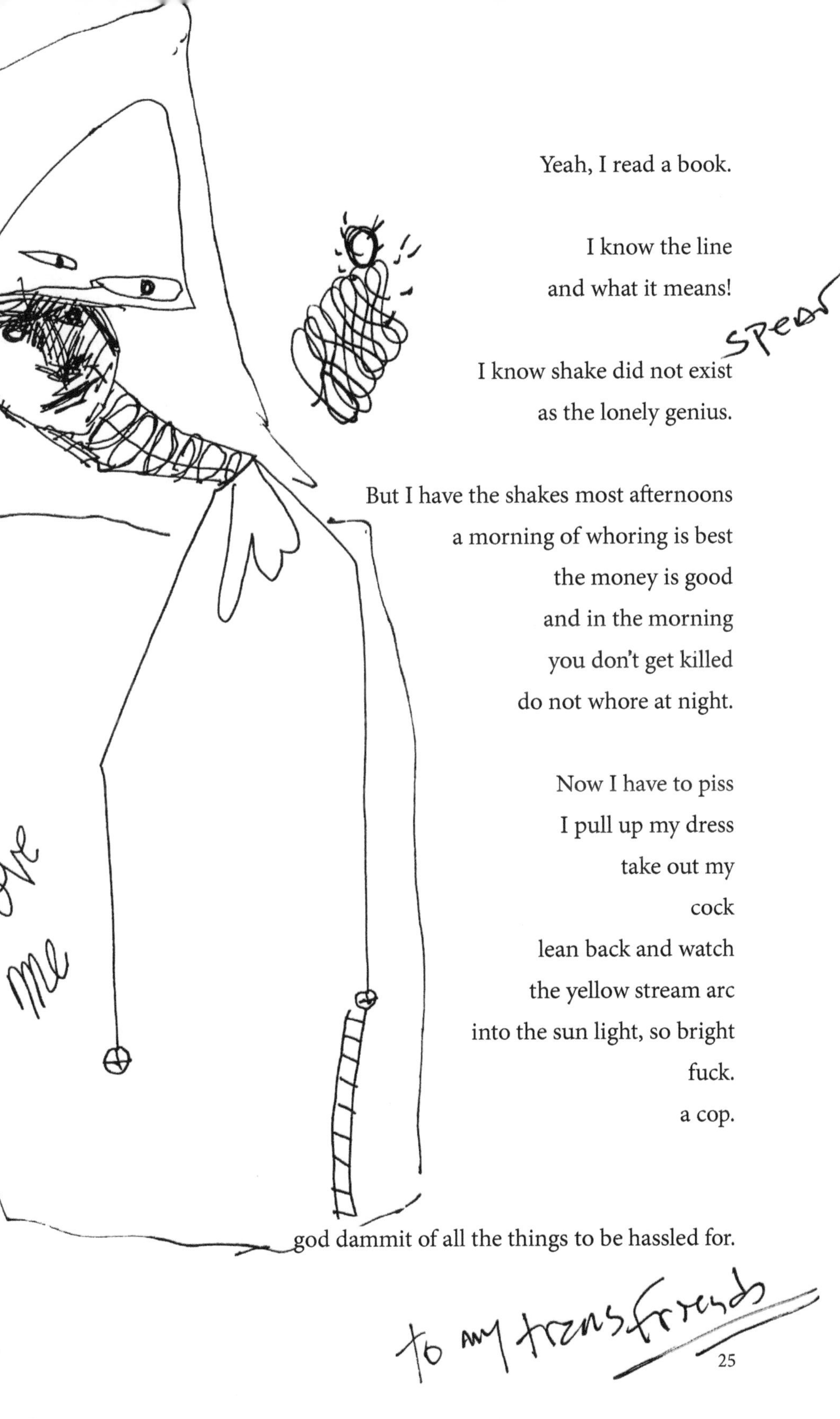

Yeah, I read a book.

I know the line
and what it means!

I know shake did not exist
as the lonely genius.

But I have the shakes most afternoons
a morning of whoring is best
the money is good
and in the morning
you don't get killed
do not whore at night.

Now I have to piss
I pull up my dress
take out my
cock
lean back and watch
the yellow stream arc
into the sun light, so bright
fuck.
a cop.

god dammit of all the things to be hassled for.

BAR FIGHT

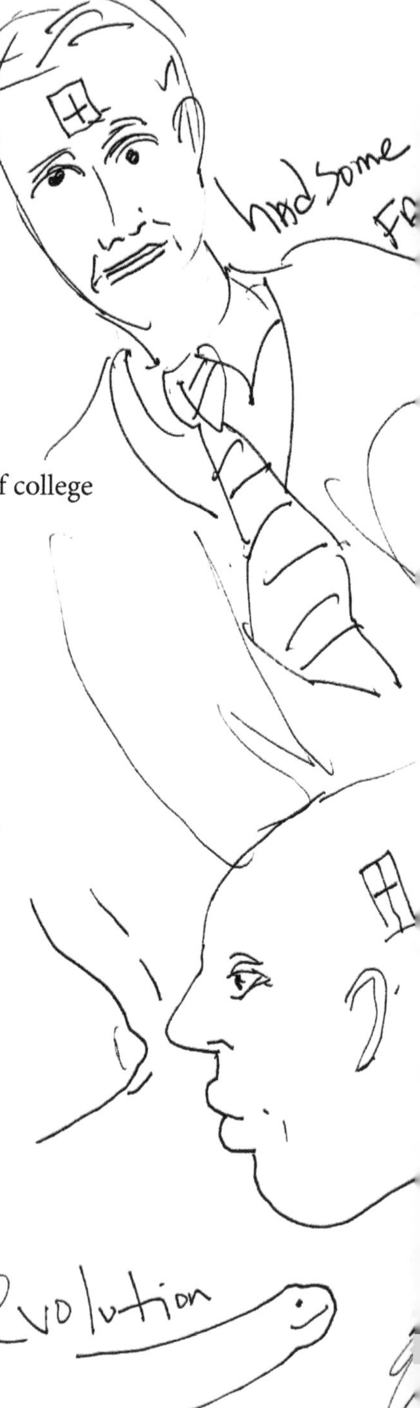

Paying their salaries
the representatives of democracy
white men with pursed lips, no lips
drained of color, a tight little club.

I am a red-blooded American boy
owe more than I can make after 4 years of college
so much thought for such a dinky job
nights spent making that stuff called art
purchased by hipsters.

Where are the Union organizers now
the poetry of steal and sweat
read with meaning by those in hard hats?

Chicago is long gone.

I saw a fight in a strip bar.
The bouncer waited till the poor asshole
was reeling drunk and grabbing
foolishly at the girls
they threw him out
beat the shit out of him
kicked his gut and face.

He was dead to this world
when I put him in the boot of my car
dropped him on the sidewalk
at the emergency room door entrance.

Drove off.

The sun was just coming up east of Troost
red clouds in the morning a sailors warning.

Most things never change.

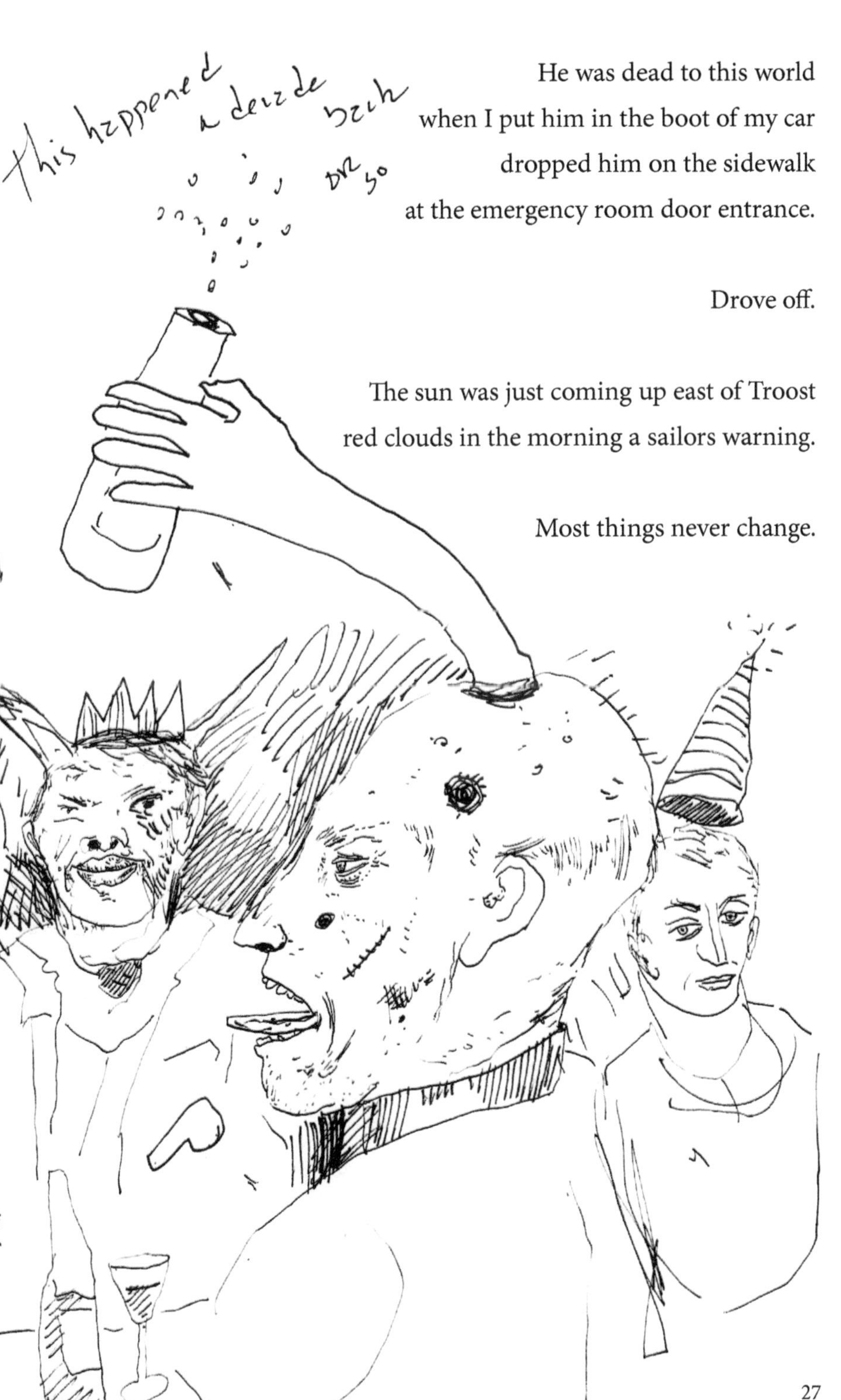

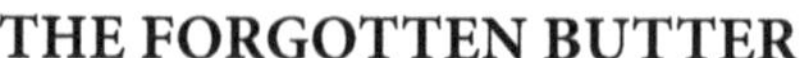

THE FORGOTTEN BUTTER

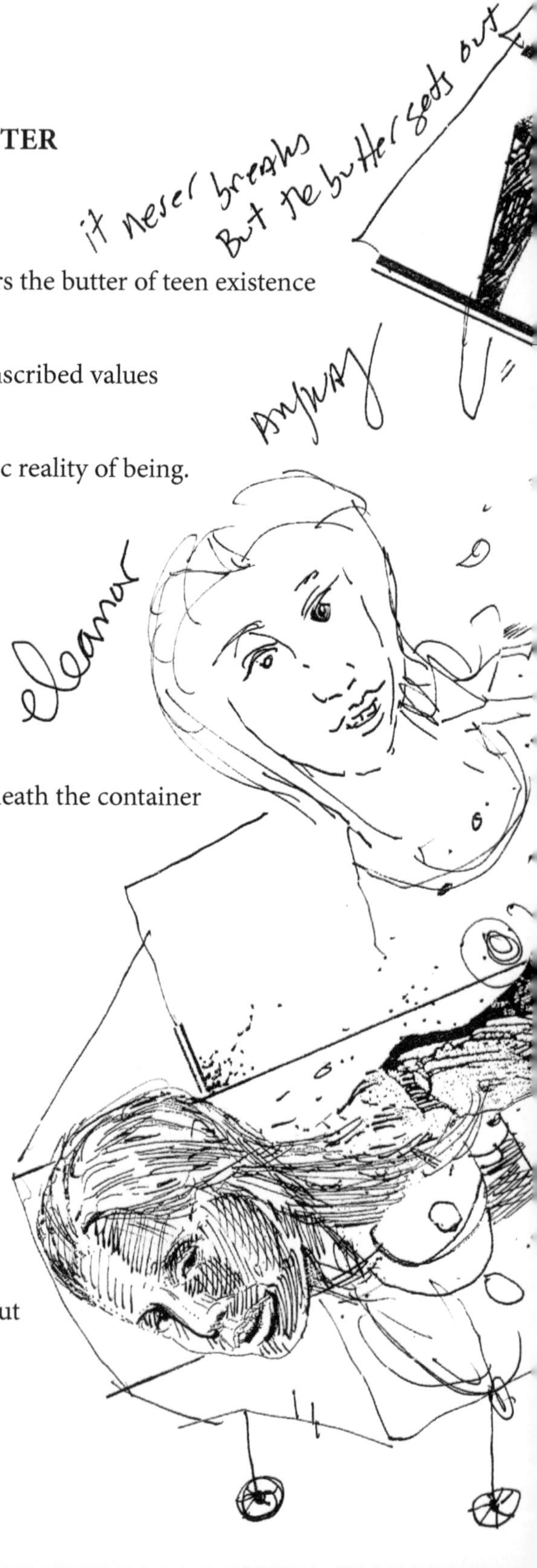

The cut glass dome that covers the butter of teen existence
is sure to break
its perfection of clarity and inscribed values
to shatter
it is no container for the erotic reality of being.
The sun
the window in Alabama
July
the forgotten butter
under the covering of glass
a solid turned to mush
then liquid running from beneath the container
free of constraints
race, sex, standards.
It becomes individuality.
One individual.
Small, meaningless?
A human?
So important
so filled with life
that all that matters
beyond the soul, beyond self
is the remember of hanging out
with you.

it never breaks
But the butter gets out
Anyway

eleanor

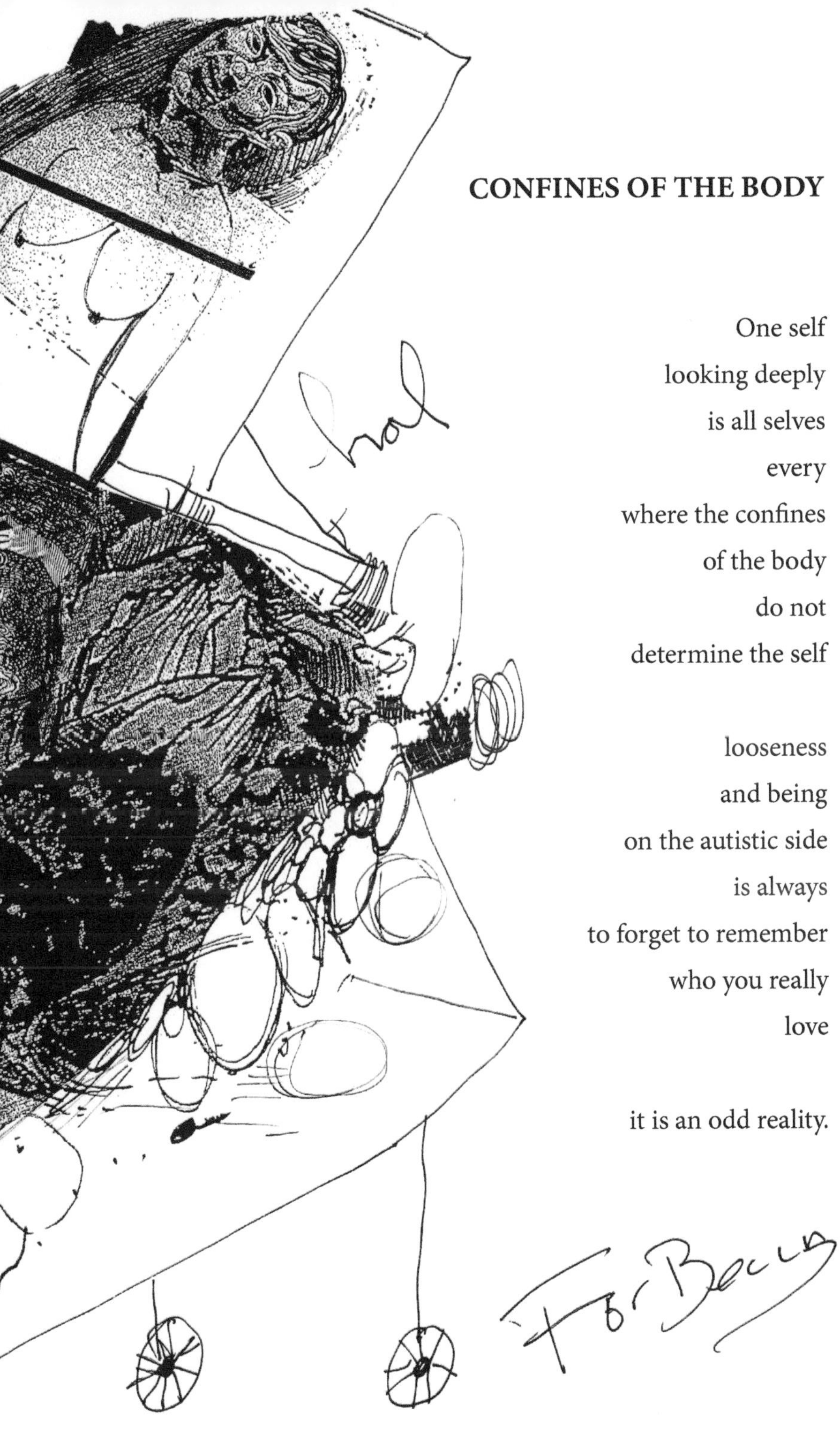

CONFINES OF THE BODY

One self
looking deeply
is all selves
every
where the confines
of the body
do not
determine the self

looseness
and being
on the autistic side
is always
to forget to remember
who you really
love

it is an odd reality.

LIVING IN CUBBY HOLES

Putting your dick in a prostitute
is a dangerous assumption
and a worst reality
but it is all I have on the 15th of each month.

Your best moment
a voice whispered in the night
wake to find it is a dream
thank god I am alone.

Do not like others intruding on my space, fear or sweet sleep.
It's a consciousness raising kind of thing I was told in therapy.

A kind of fear of intimacy
always having to be the actor
it makes one puke sooner or later.

Alone it does not matter.

There is just me and my kindness
roared off into the world
my dad said
you are free, white and 18
get out.

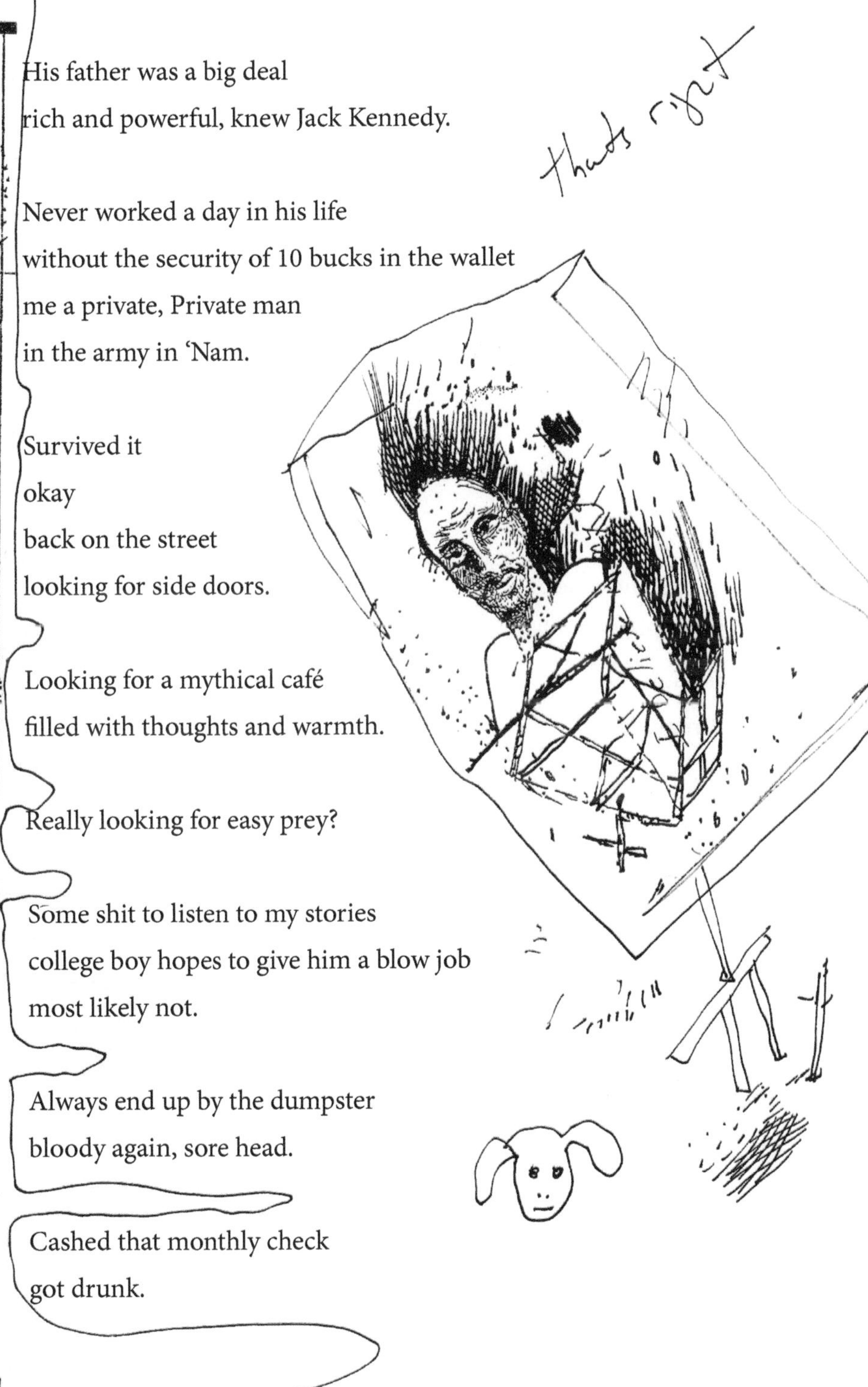

His father was a big deal
rich and powerful, knew Jack Kennedy.

Never worked a day in his life
without the security of 10 bucks in the wallet
me a private, Private man
in the army in 'Nam.

Survived it
okay
back on the street
looking for side doors.

Looking for a mythical café
filled with thoughts and warmth.

Really looking for easy prey?

Some shit to listen to my stories
college boy hopes to give him a blow job
most likely not.

Always end up by the dumpster
bloody again, sore head.

Cashed that monthly check
got drunk.

Then robbed
just like last month.

The deserving poor?

A war hero
a bum in the half-way house
a half-ass poet pretending to write.

No.
Just a client
on a fixed income
dead at 46
Maryland Ave.
Baltimore MD
1973.

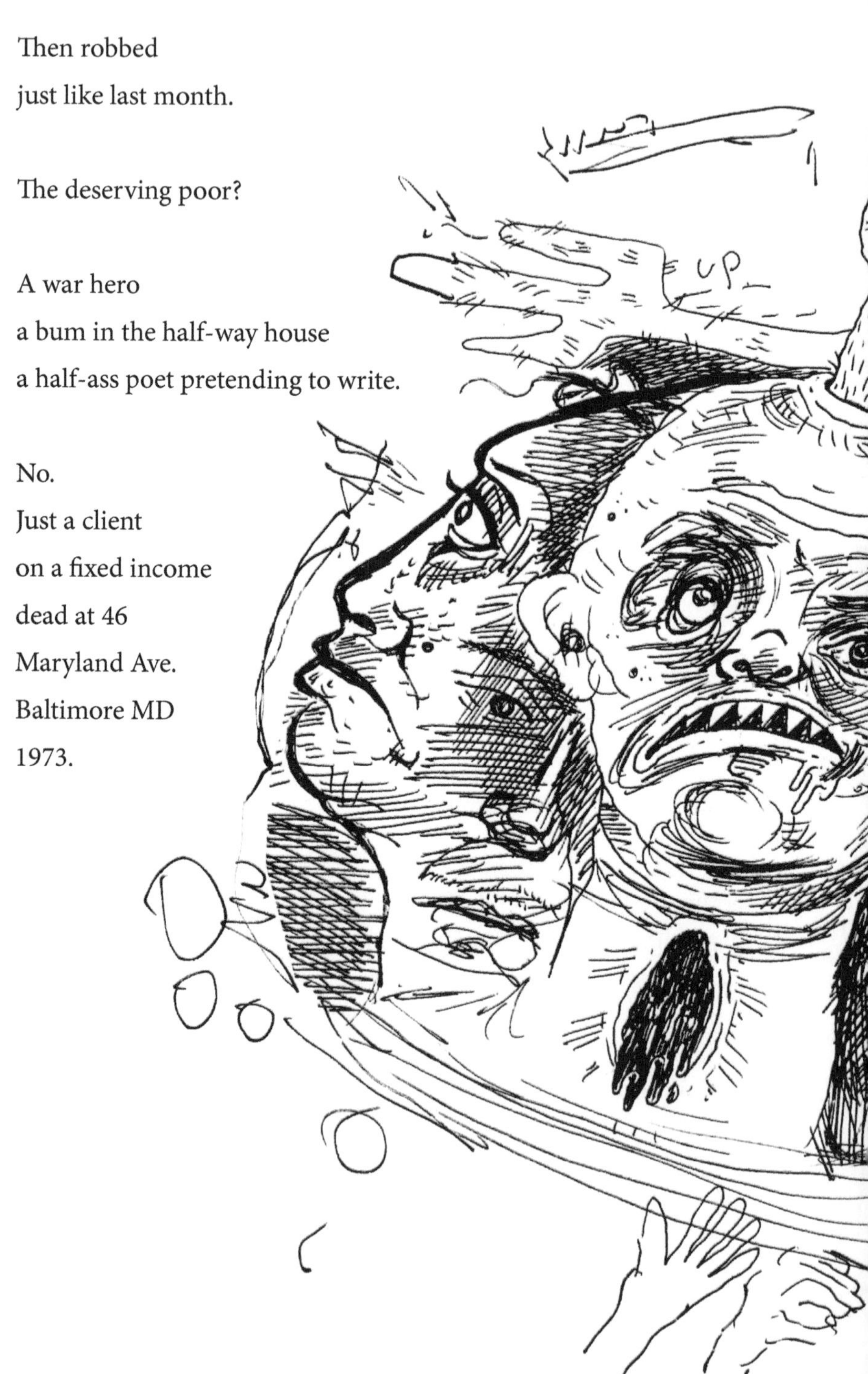

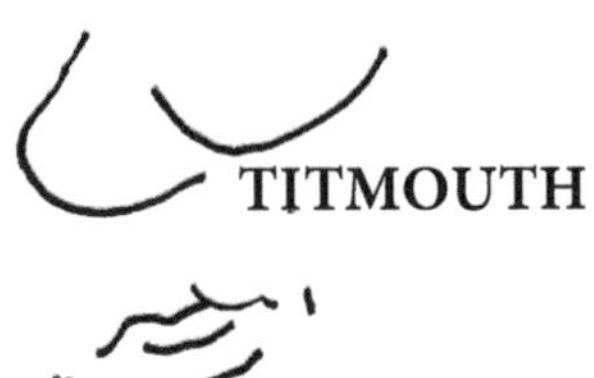

TITMOUTH

The breasts I consumed had no identity.
They existed outside of intimacy.
I puked Gerber's out
as quickly as it was
pushed down my throat.

A thousand years later
in another life
bearing my teeth
I take the tit in my mouth.

The bite of pleasure and pain
laughing, yelling, slapping
we are one
you push ideas through my lips
and I am beyond
self-invention
beyond insolences.

I can only grunt incoherently.
I am for once truly alive
sleeping as a child in your soul.

THINK UP

the poems are not
in my head
they pass through my head
or brain or mine
but do not stay

I do not remember
them
what they are about
or even that I wrote them

you sent back one
and I thought you had written it
till I saw a line that made me remember it was mine

my experience is in each
but it is also outside of me
passes through me
is not something I think up

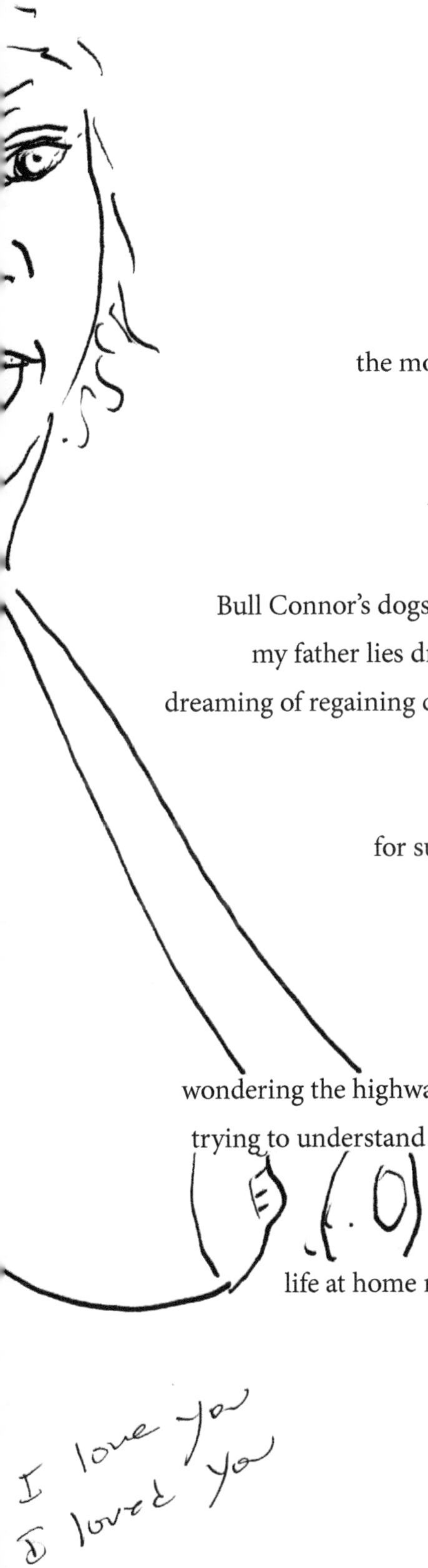

CLARITY

the extraordinary stillness
the monk on TV bursts into flames in Saigon
I watched him char
on the black and white television
while others are fire-hosed in Alabama

Bull Connor's dogs rip their skin and tear off their clothes
my father lies drunk in his darkened bedroom at noon
dreaming of regaining control of these lost city states of power

how does a 16-year-old stand up
for such inflammatory messages of defiance
what is the life of a *this boy*
already addicted to beer, sex, TV
to seething boredom

wondering the highways by night in a red convertible Impala
trying to understand the radio tuned to symphonic music at
90 miles an hour

life at home reduced to a series of heated arguments
over insignificant decisions

learning always to go for the jugular

a punch thrown true
and another combustible fist fight

I lived in a middle class
all white community
of course

but haunted the *Negro Streets* (as Ginsberg said) hung out in DC
and the Howard Theatre for 5 bucks: tickets for Etta James, the
Temptations, Smokie, James Brown, Wicked Wilson Picket

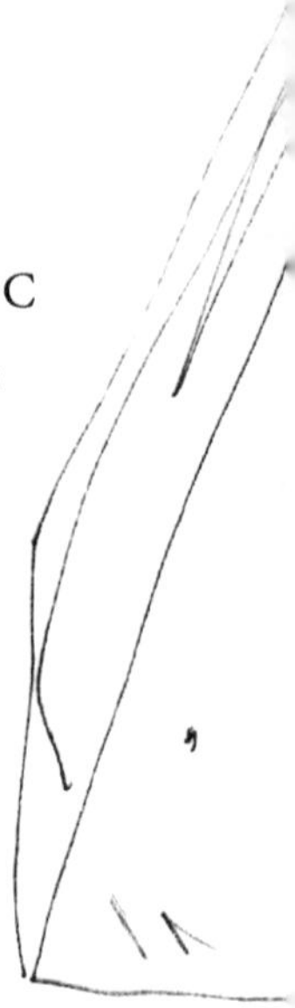

they tore out their souls for us

tore them out
and placed them in our hearts
these black men/women
their songs
saving a rich white boy
even I could see the enormous symbolic significance

a people oppressed torn apart laying down such music from
Miles to Coltrane, the Supremes to Stax, they built visionary
worlds, temples of passion, grace and peace

doling out soul powers from the bitterness of civil rights denied
simple rights long time scrawled on paper, revoked, ignored
from rights denied and derailed, came the art that

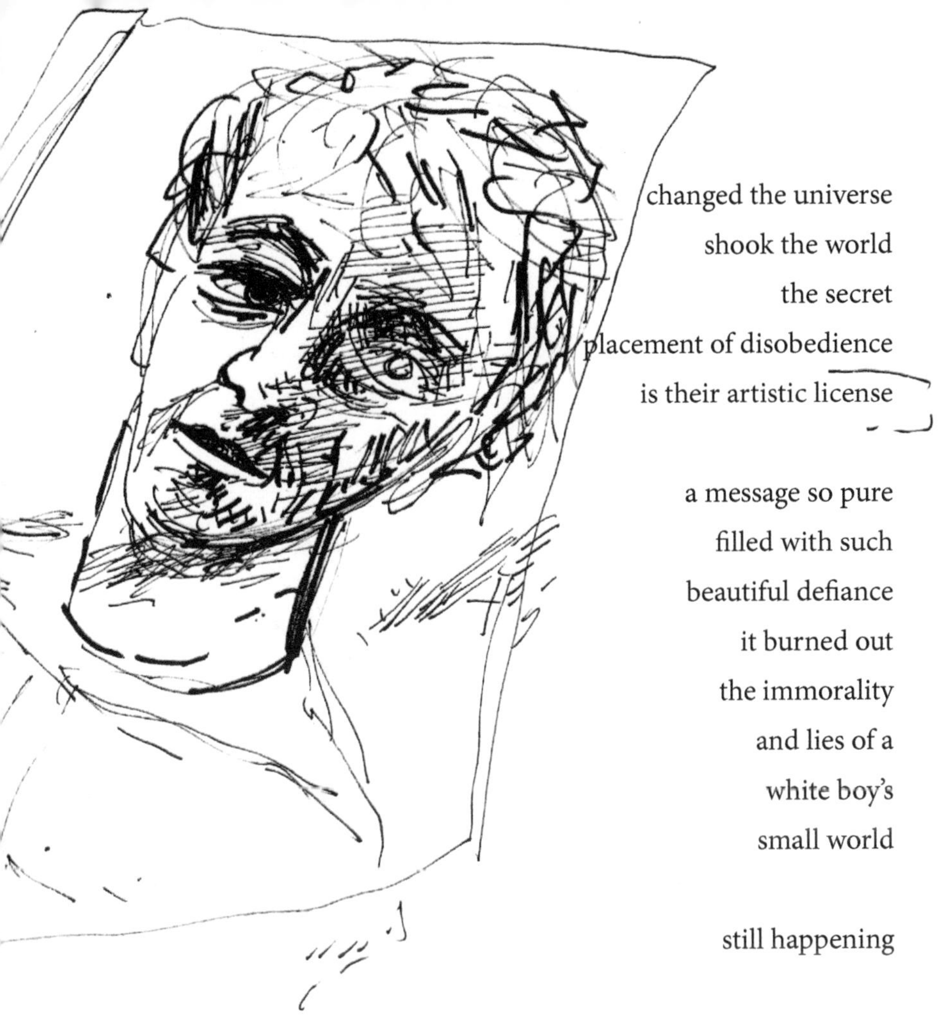

changed the universe
shook the world
the secret
placement of disobedience
is their artistic license

a message so pure
filled with such
beautiful defiance
it burned out
the immorality
and lies of a
white boy's
small world

still happening

both the oppression and the saving

there would be perhaps 18 white folks—kids—in the audience
for James Brown, but if you had the balls to go up to the Howard
Theatre (and were respectful), it was tolerated, even celebrated

Bullet history
over and over again

(then
king
was
killed)

A BAD SIGN

Her period had begun on Sunday.
A bad sign.
Sucking a beer she collapses.
The dance of the weeping is just beginning.
The coffee is hot and he is not aware of the open door.

The cold wind is as rain.

Birds no longer perch near the entrance.
A bad sign.
A face wet with the mist
of a thousand oceans
breaks the plane of the warmth.
Weeping
tired of her body
tired of her mind.

Everything is more than nothing.

A memory.

Always a judgment.
Next. Next. Next. Next.

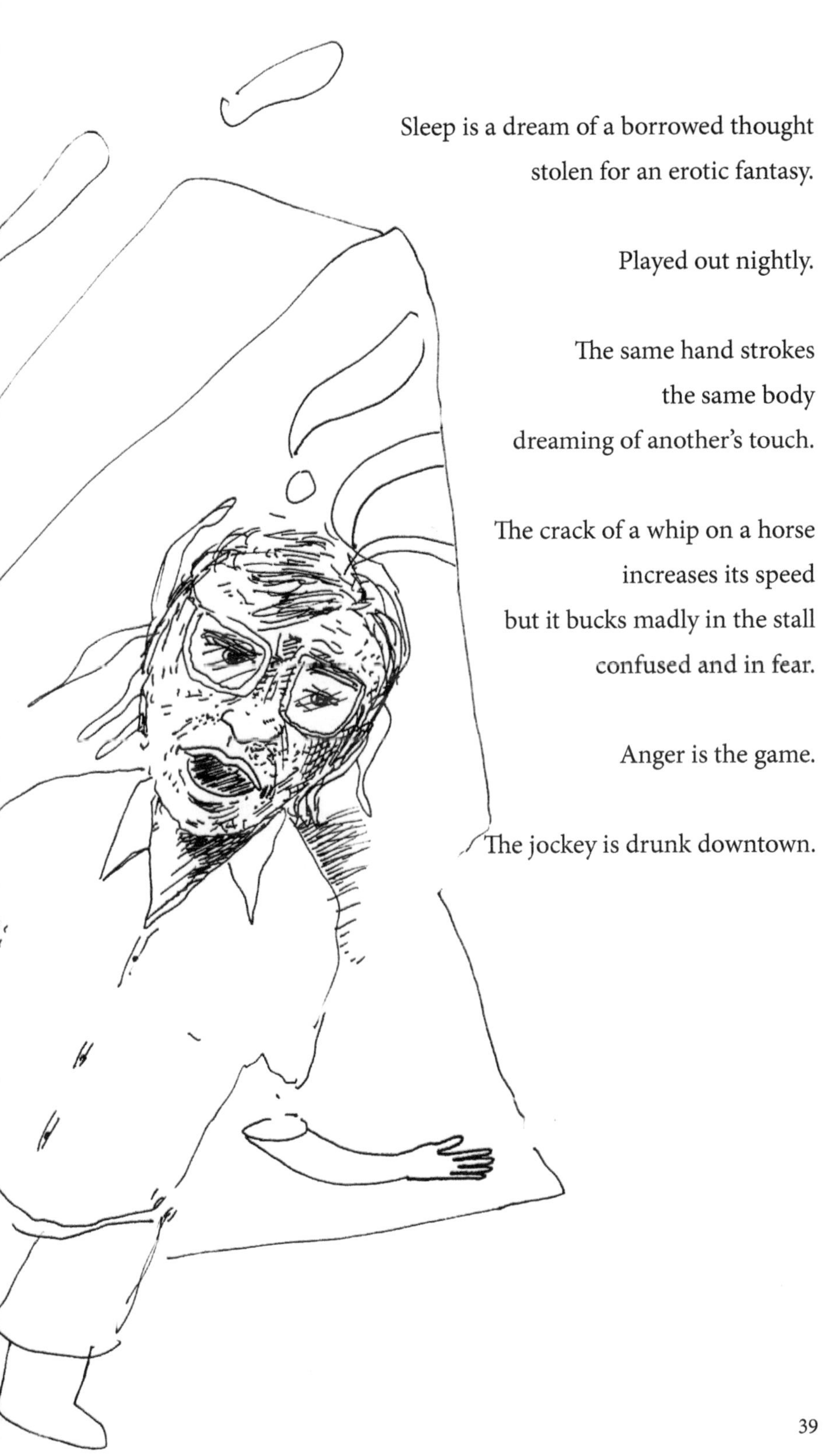

Sleep is a dream of a borrowed thought
stolen for an erotic fantasy.

Played out nightly.

The same hand strokes
the same body
dreaming of another's touch.

The crack of a whip on a horse
increases its speed
but it bucks madly in the stall
confused and in fear.

Anger is the game.

The jockey is drunk downtown.

DROP DRIP

Jordan watched the plasma drip.
The air bubble ready to enter his vein -- -- -- -o- -- body.

Now nothing brings me to you.

And if it did, I am not wanted
I am a memory of past joy? your second life?
Forgotten of course
the fucking like wild dogs.

Joy, oh joy, turned to indifference
no thoughts for tomorrow
no *each other.*

Now only space and dreams
despair, emptiness
quickly dismissed as the past
illusions of pain, a silly dream

-- -- -- -- -- -- transitory -- -- -- -o- --

calling out
balance the boat
I don't care.

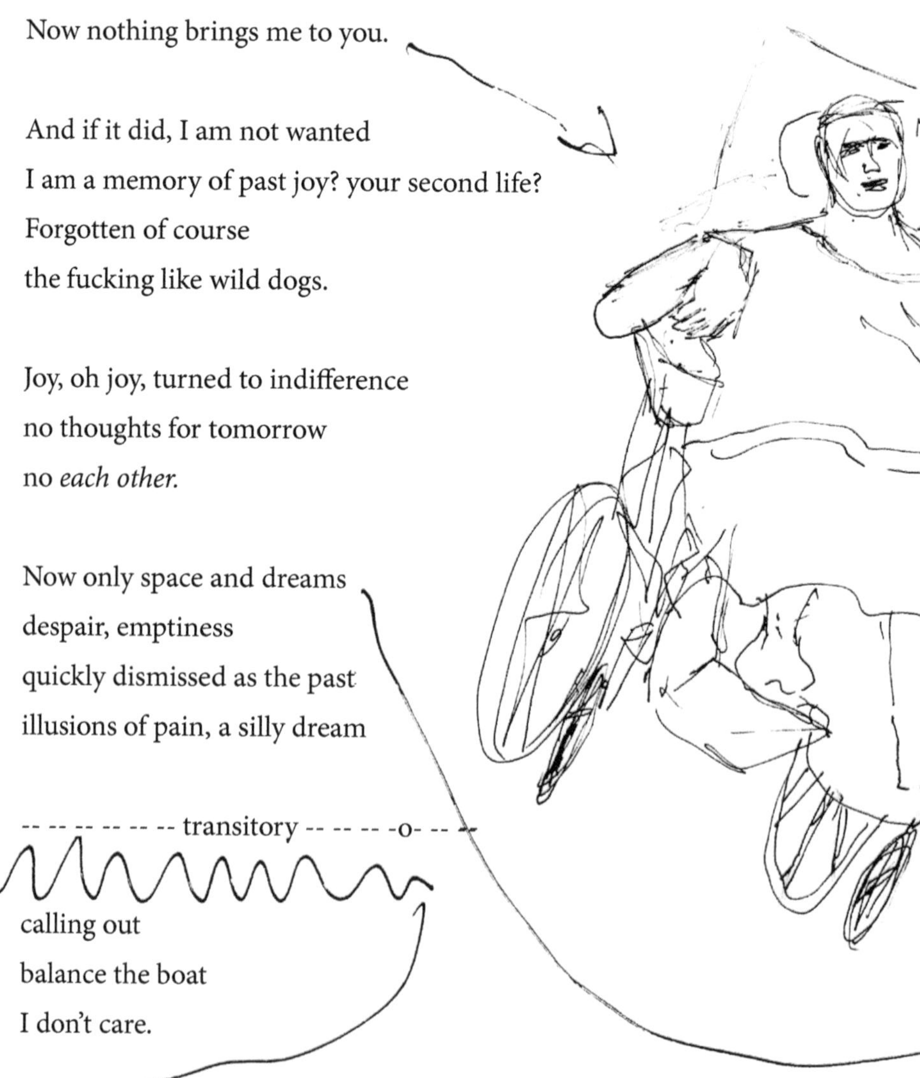

Like a poor ones voyage
little can be carried down
the long ramp.

The soldiers came
they game down this road
flows seemed to form:

voluptuous
soil, neolithic
sinuous fertility
eminently desirable
the dream of abundance.

The soldiers came
they game down this road.
All is destroyed.
Now fixed in time
as a knowable concept
peace
a piece to be retrieved
never again knowing.

-- -- -- -o- -- -- -- -- -- -- -- -- -- -- -- *Exquisite erotic actuality.*

POGROMS OF DELIGHT

criminal deeds that never culminate at dawn
the adventurer's last venture
a crime, but no tall prison walls for the guilty
for the wealthy, no oppression
divisibility gamblers, Carpathian generals
selling secret shapes on shorelines, always divine
reckless perspicacity
never allowing, an indisputable identity
never itself rigorously one (won)
but indisputably something
an abhorrent estuary in the desert
now so dry
these pogroms of delight
the notorious always smiling
failing examinations for the luckless, the listless
no compass to show the place of the ancient murders
guided by the unfamiliar jewelry of midnight stars
unlucky victims looking across the hall to a blaze
of white culture splendor turned fragrant

crossing an ancient sea of sweat
a life turned violently rotten
culminating in resignation
that this boat will not reach the shore

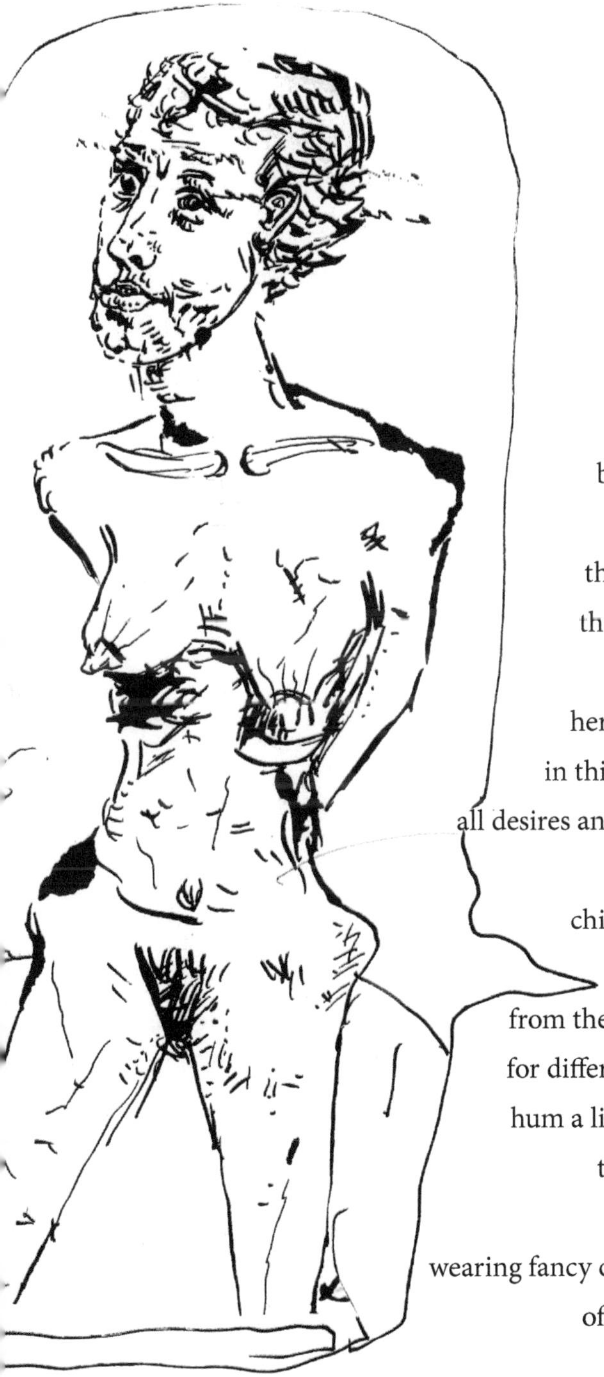

TRANSIT

this unknown place
that fosters no bias
a trench that recognizes
no one's body
this mass of humanity
lies broken
bent arms to broken faces

this is an unreadable guide
this is a guide to separating
nothing
here no repackaged wisdom
in this a secluded place, where
all desires and thoughts are combined
with earth and clay
children play on green grass
each spring well fed
from the souls of those murdered
for difference, ideals and progress
hum a little song for repossessing
the unclaimed in my time
when it was my turn
wearing fancy clothes, I missed the train
of unbuttoned appearances

HUM

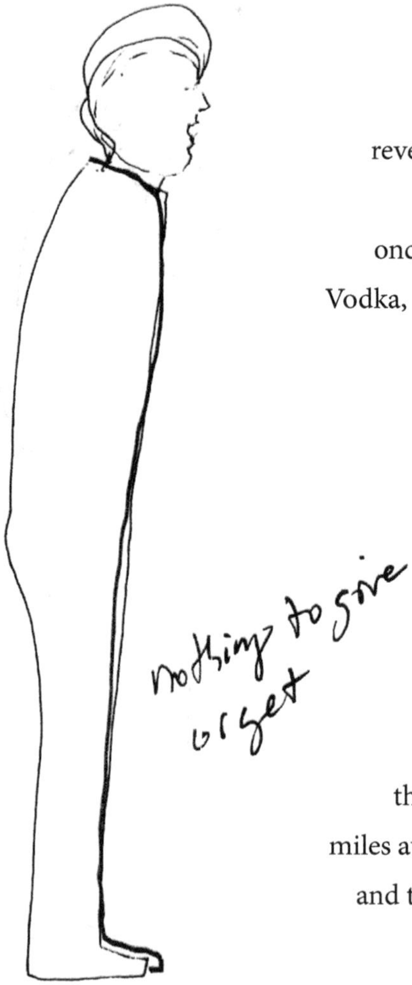

from the café comes tango
reverberations under the bridge
the sleeping man
once at the breast of his mother
Vodka, Christ, my Buddha, all gone

bells from the church

silent

the passing blast of the ghetto
miles away the air is moved by hate
and the hum lands in Manhattan
shards of breaking glass
the tinkling of one another
zero in on flames
iron infused dust eats at the concrete
the pond is rippled
distant cycles, it begins again
repair

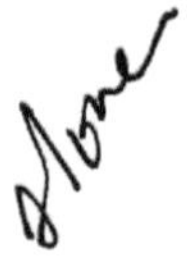

make noise, gesticulate, try to breathe
can Johnny come out to play baseball?

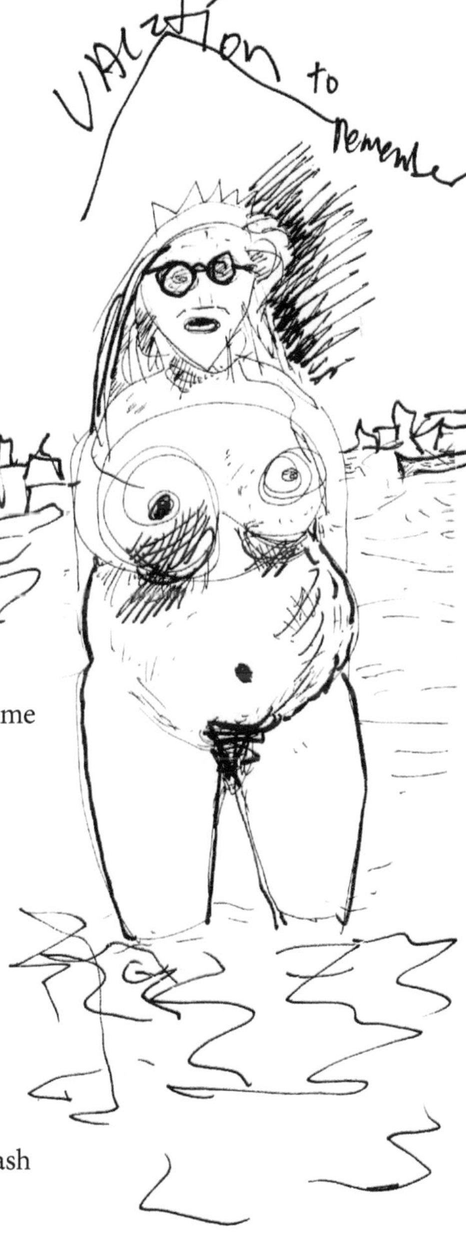

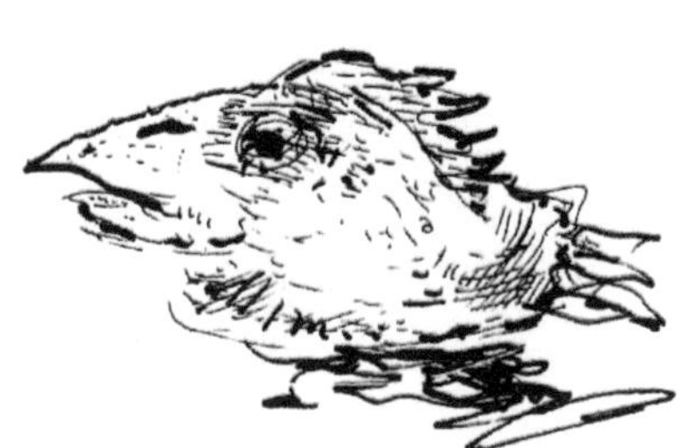

no

we give back to all or our customers
it's not a bad deal
make money
a little scam on Saturday afternoons
eliminate your debts, your auto loans
term reducer
payment program
credit cards and mortgages
the smell of sweat, piss, sperm and perfume
behind the dumpster
the tire is off, flat and the hole is broken

can't be fixed

how can a whole be broken?
for god sakes it's only a hole
30% discount and the air is getting cold
the sun sets behind the foreclosed car wash
we walk home the deal undone

JUST A CERTAIN KIND OF HELL

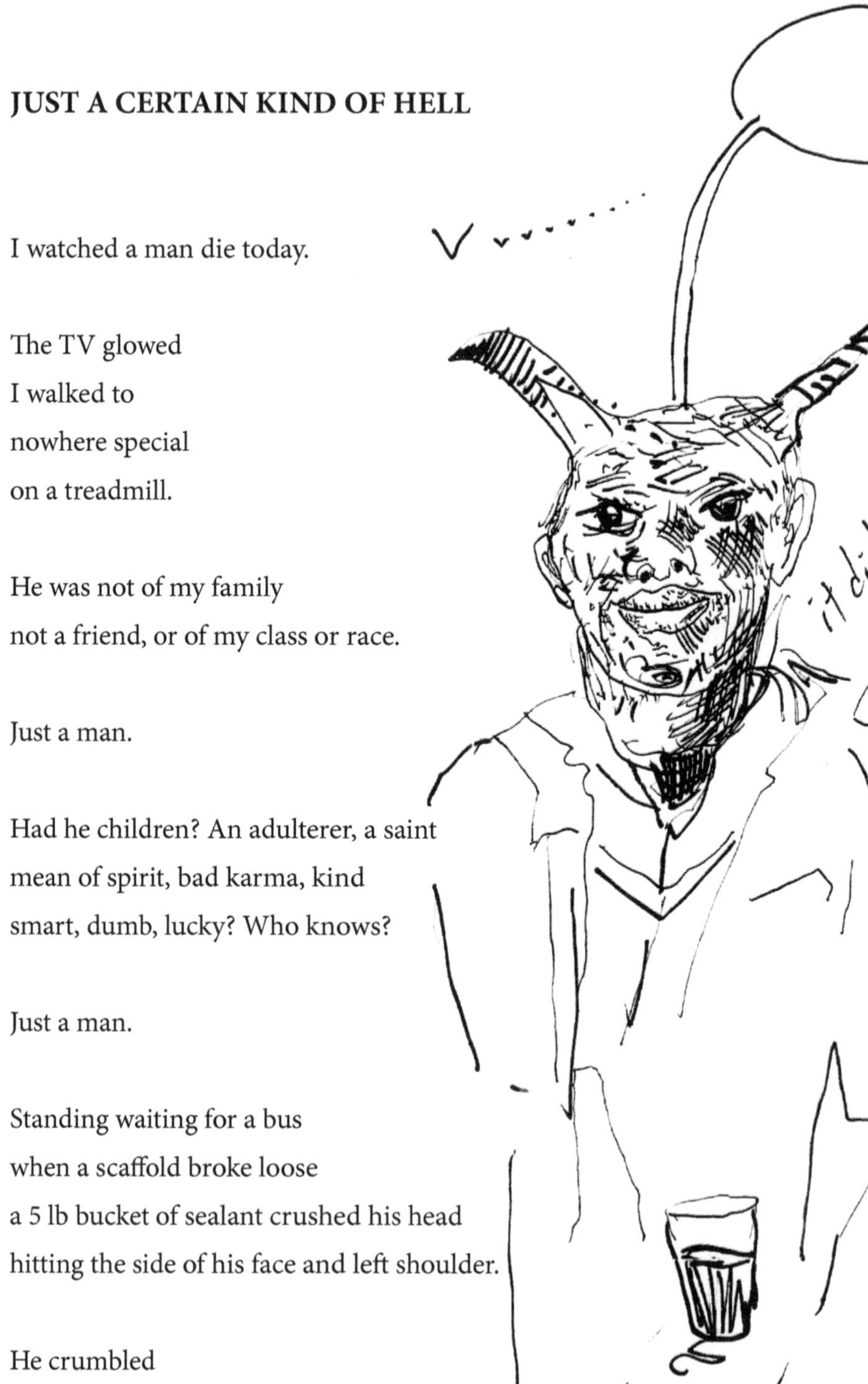

I watched a man die today.

The TV glowed
I walked to
nowhere special
on a treadmill.

He was not of my family
not a friend, or of my class or race.

Just a man.

Had he children? An adulterer, a saint
mean of spirit, bad karma, kind
smart, dumb, lucky? Who knows?

Just a man.

Standing waiting for a bus
when a scaffold broke loose
a 5 lb bucket of sealant crushed his head
hitting the side of his face and left shoulder.

He crumbled

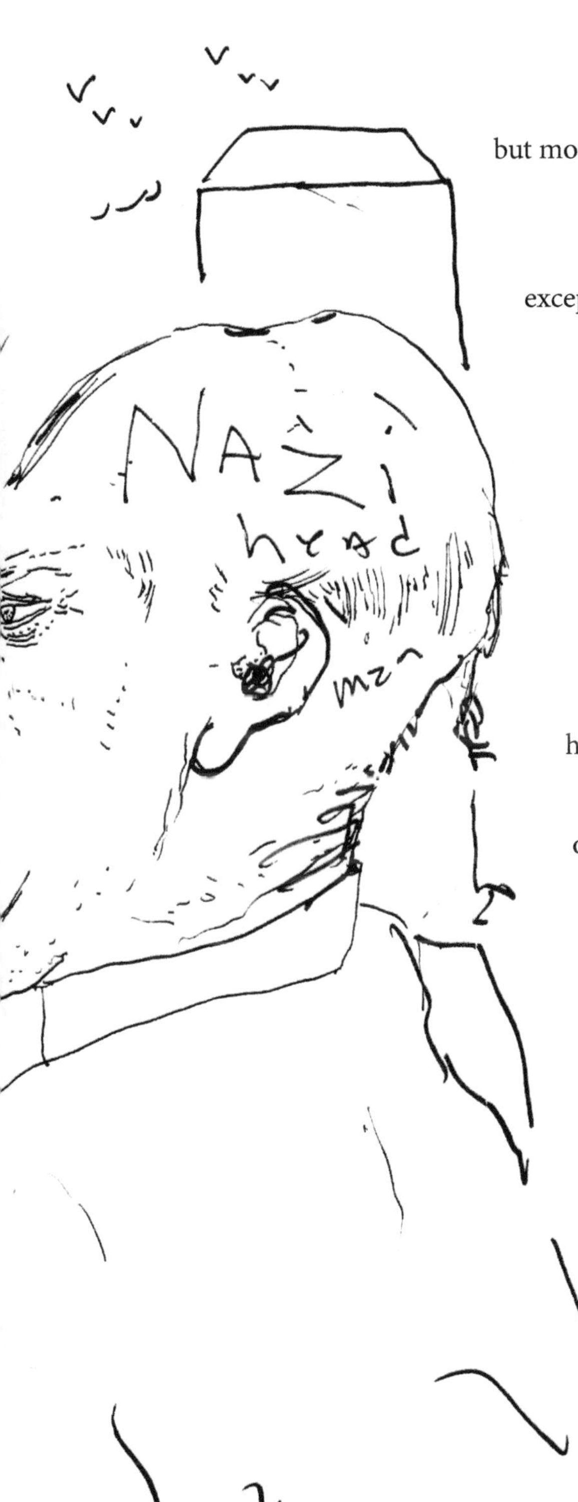

not like a human
but more like a cartoon character.

It was slightly funny
except for the false caring faces
of the talking heads
and then the replay
in slow motion
recycling sad faces.

And a commercial -- -- -.

His death is over
his moment of fame is gone
unless it is funny
or weird enough to be a hit
on YouTube.

Mmm
2 mile mark
and the game
is coming up
after the weather.

I saw a man die today.

RING AROUNDS

Ring arounds are clothes,
they are the uniforms given to prisoners in the south,

in ole Alabama and Mississippi, in the Jim Crow 1930s.
Both colored and white

prisoners wore ring arounds when they locked them up
for vagrancy.

There was a white man from Dothen, Alabama, he was known
to walk the straight

and narrow, a God fearing Baptist. His first memory was of
working another man's

fields and now at 53 it was the only life he knew. He couldn't read,
but he could see

the world around him and he knew being poor was a life
sentence, and to be colored

and poor a crime -- -- -- -- with real time to do,-- -- -- -- -- --
no doubt about it.

When the sun was high overhead, and his day in the field was not yet half finished,

he always thought he could smell the sea. He had never seen the
Gulf of Mexico, but

he had seen a small picture of it in the house of a man he cut
wood for. The painting

was of a beach with boats and sea birds flying in the setting sun.
Naked red neck,

a scalded white body that never saw the sun, burnt face, dirty
burnt hands,

no socks only handed down brogans, bug-bitten in the summer
and cold in the winter,

kids 9, wives 2, jailed for being young with drunkenness,
fighting and burning down his shack,

the one owned by another man. Now, he was broke down.
He had worked quietly,

without pity, or joy, no long thoughts or spoken complaints. He
was buried on the other man's

ground, in November, that mean month of 1951, finally
a free man.

BONES

No one looked down on the rain-washed granite face
where the trees rotted and fell.
The tire in the gully was all that was left
intact of the 1949 Buick that had left the
road so long ago.

Above, at the overlook, a couple
held their baby high, arms stretched, blond hair
sparkling in the Colorado sunshine.

The elderly couple stepped from their mobile home
and waved at the clouds, pre-teens moped
in the back seats of cars
playing video games
never looking up at the
purple/orange mountain ridge.

A local cursed the tourist traffic
as he crept down the mountain to take his kids
bowling.

Over the ridge, in chorus with the chirping
of mountain larks a motorcycle whined
up the pass from the valley floor 8 miles away.

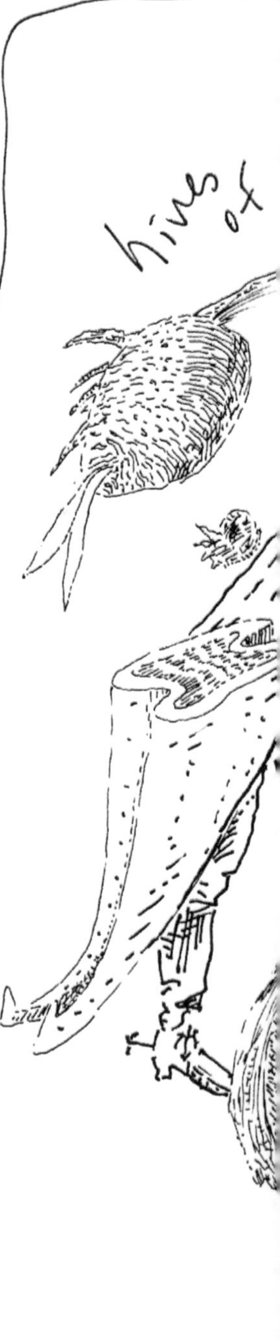

Notes to J.P.

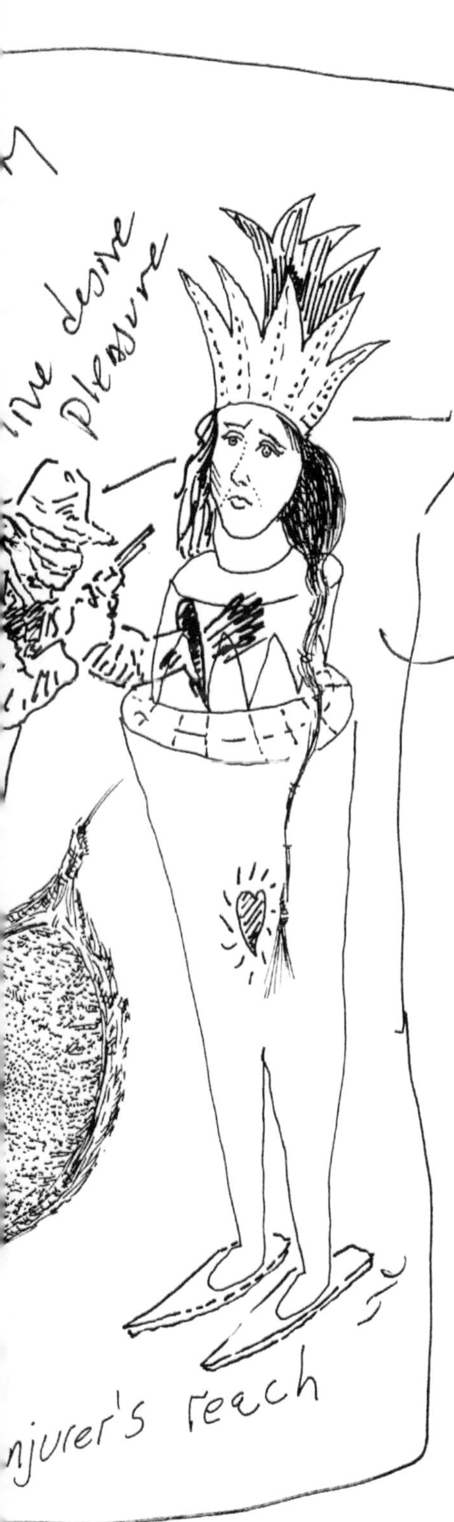

The poem relates
to the way we sit on the land
and are not part of it; it is as if for
locals, visitors
and even those who fly over
that the mountains
are a backdrop for their
lives, desires and pleasures,
as artificial as a pro bass
fishing lure or a plastic worm.

That we cannot reach
the meaning of the land
we stare at
and cannot be part of its
nature is as old as society itself.

Ask those elders
that die
on Easter Island
Chaco Canyon
Times Beach.

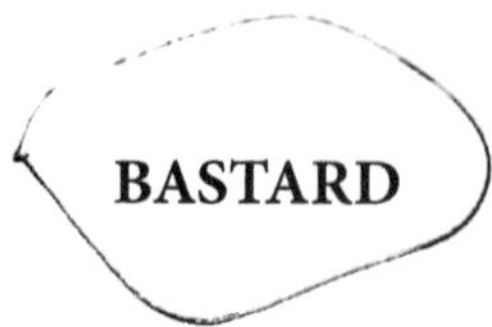

BASTARD

I saw Stevie Wonder piss in a urinal.
It was 1967: the bar, The Journeys Inn
a small club and
I had to piss
just prior to Wonder going on stage.

I ran into the men's room
stood next to him pulled out my penis and
yes I looked. Stared in fact. Because I knew he did not care.
He did not know I was staring
he couldn't see a thing.

And yes, he was big.

My stream stopped before his and I made it back to the bar.
My mother was not married and my brother was an only child.
He did not know that my father had fucked his brother's wife.
It all came to light much later.
I was almost grown by then.

Dratsab was my nickname
but I was dyslexic so I got the joke quickly.

My mother reigned over bitter times

looking out on a back yard of rubbish and uncut grass.
Depending on who had access to her rather beautiful body
the yard improved or fell further into disrepair.

Blues songs were a fitting
background, wailing and singing.
I love that big black 10-inch,
big black 10-inch record of the blues.
The soundtrack for this dysfunctional home and its balding yard
where new paths were fashioned
by the ever present running and barking dogs.
Most did not stay long enough to get a name.
It was insane for grass to even try to grow there.

I left after my first year of high school
and traveled north to Washington, DC.

Black 10 inch of the Record that plays the Blues

The day I left she was watching
a portable black and white TV.
Lucy was working in the pie factory.
The more she hurried
the more the pies fell to the factory floor.

My mom laughed
I guess she saw her self, her life, in that frantic comedian.
A life that was always out of control
with things coming just a little too fast.

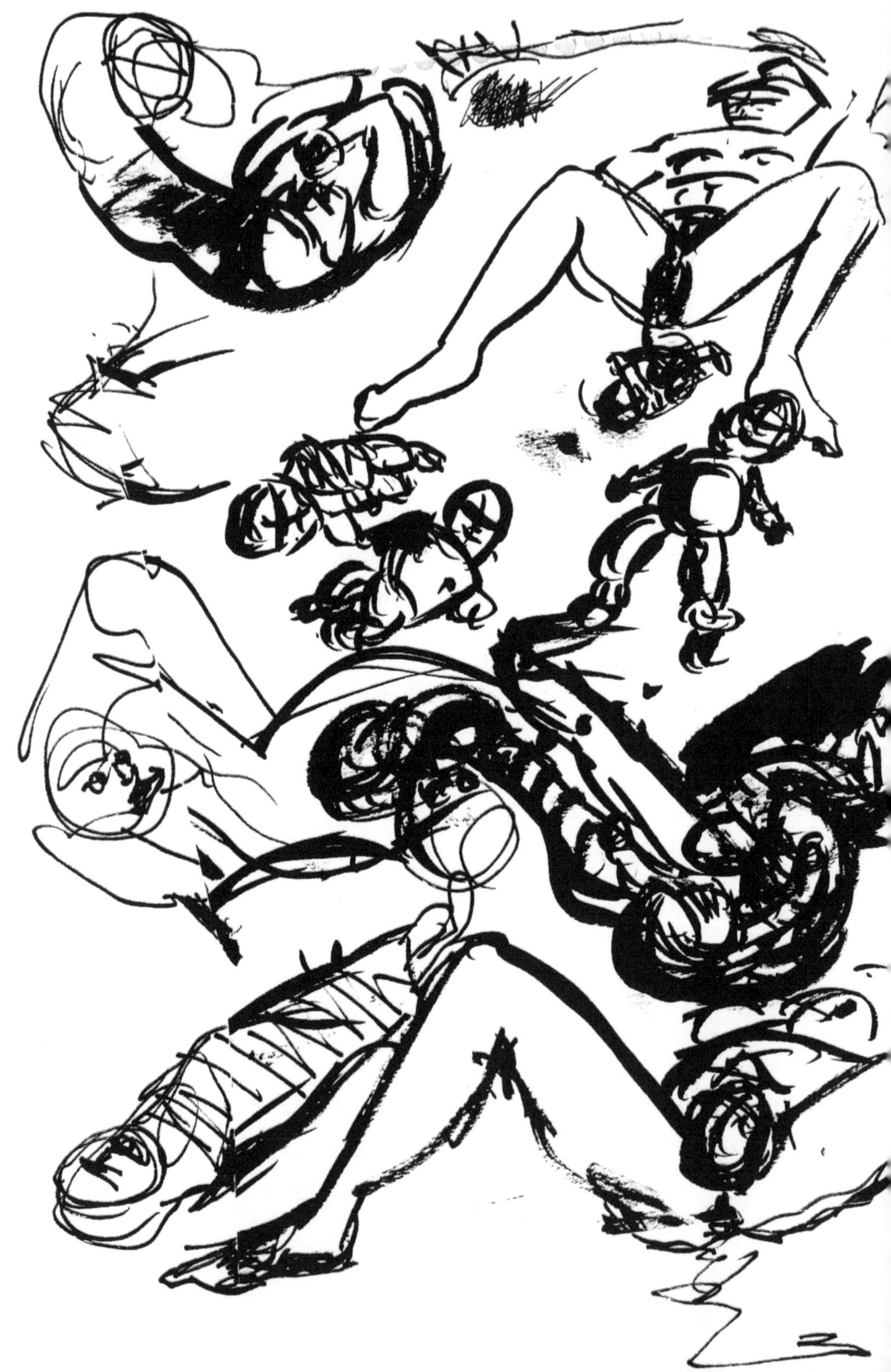

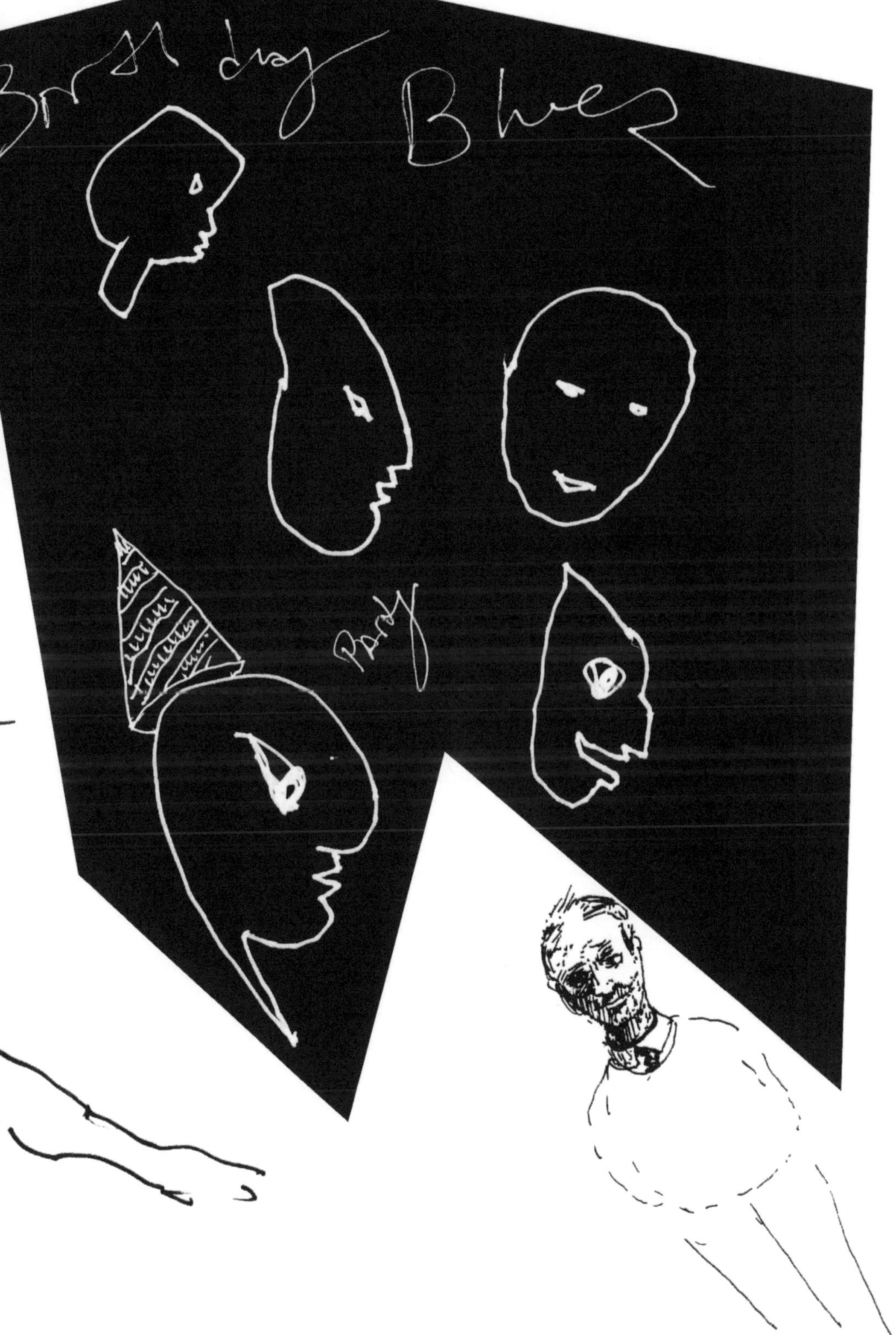
Birthday Blues
Party

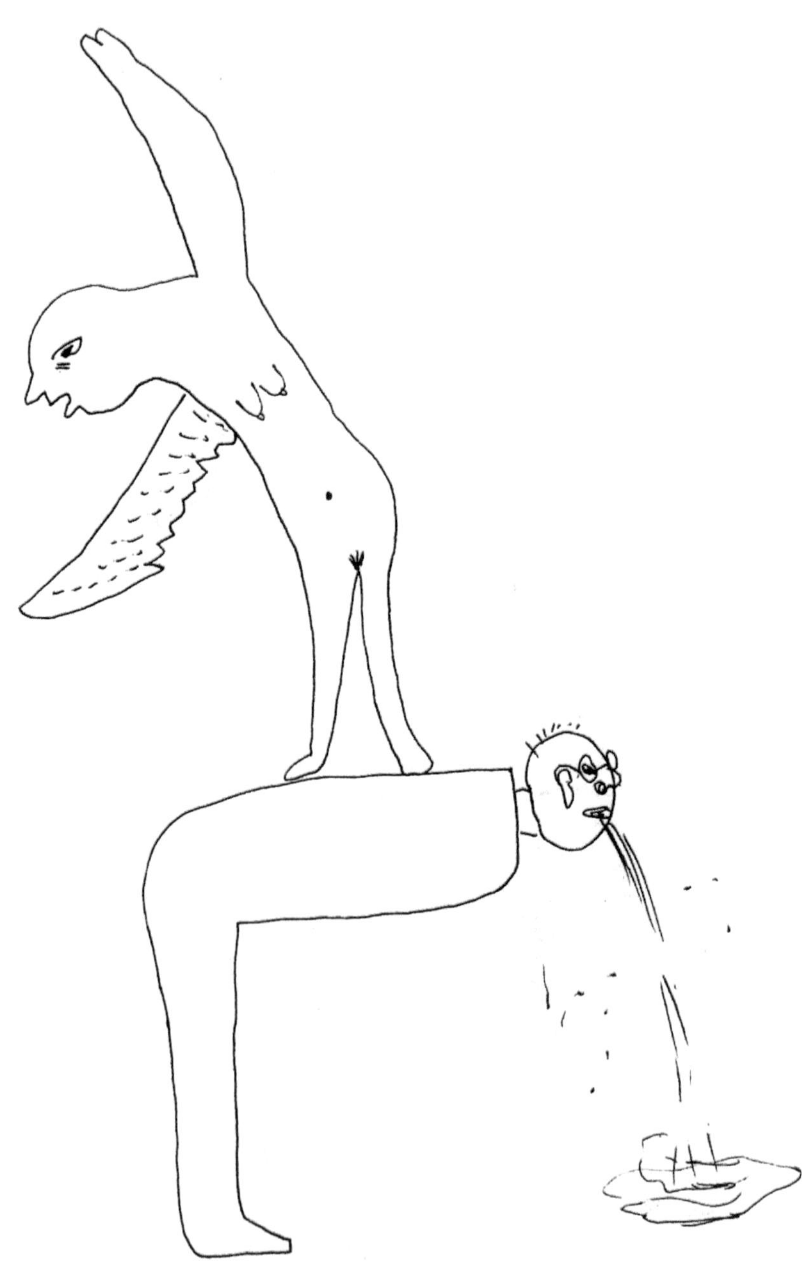

www.ingramcontent.com/pod-product-compliance
Ingram Content Group UK Ltd.
Pitfield, Milton Keynes, MK11 3LW, UK
UKHW041643190726
13854UKWH00006B/2659

9 780990 864950